Scripture Bulletin Boards for Every Season

by
Tom Orange

illustrated by Brenda Youngmeyer

Cover by Kathryn Hyndman

Shining Star Publications, Copyright © 1987

A Division of Good Apple, Inc.

ISBN No. 0-86653-397-4

Standardized Subject Code TA ac

Printing No. 987

Shining Star Publications
A Division of Good Apple, Inc.
Box 299
Carthage, IL 62321-0299

Unless otherwise indicated, the King James Version of the Bible was used in preparing the activities in this book.

TABLE OF CONTENTS

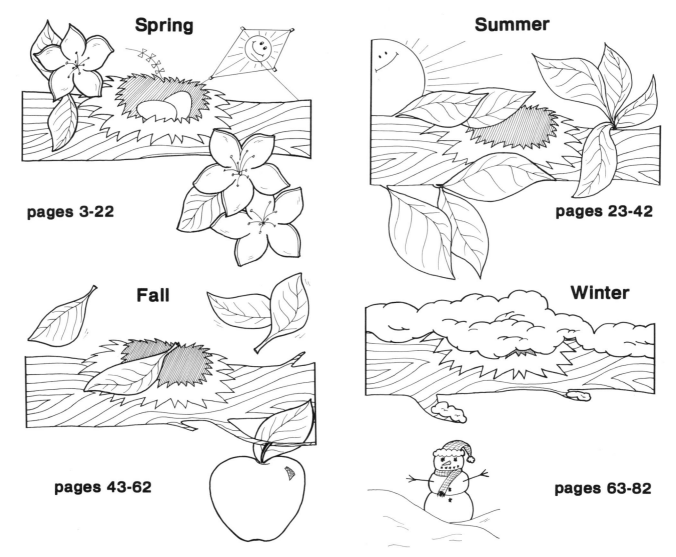

USING SCRIPTURE BULLETIN BOARDS

The book is divided into sections according to the four seasons, with each section containing suggestions for special holidays occurring during that season.

Patterns for illustrating each bulletin board are provided in the back of the book and may be used any way you wish.

An easy way of enlarging the illustrations is to use an overhead projector. Trace the pattern on some clear transparency material and then place it on your projector. Now you are ready to make your illustrations as large or as small as you desire.

May your visual representations be a blessing within your classroom and/or church. May you, the creator, also receive a blessing as you develop scriptural truths and principles through your creations.

OTHER WAYS TO USE THE ILLUSTRATIONS

- name tags
- work sheets
- class announcements
- program covers
- thank-you notes

- publication graphics
- art idea starters
- language idea starters
- and many more . . . .

2

SS1826

SPRING

Shining Star Publications, Copyright © 1987, A division of Good Apple, Inc.

SS1826

Swing into reading

DIRECTIONS:
Use a bright blue background, brown tree trunk and limb, and green leaves to make the tree for this bulletin board. For a 3-D effect, use real rope and a piece of wood 1″ × 6″ for the swing. Display Scripture verses that apply to what you're "swinging" into. This might be a good time to emphasize this year's classroom verse.

IDEAS:
Let your imagination go on this bulletin board. You might use it to display some of the children's creative writing to highlight any subject—reading, math, science, language, music, geography, spelling.

ALTERNATIVE TITLES AND SCRIPTURE VERSES:
(Reading)

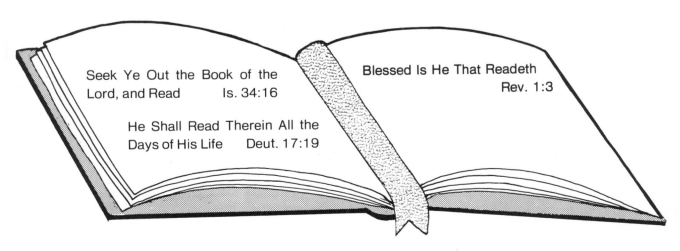

Seek Ye Out the Book of the Lord, and Read   Is. 34:16

He Shall Read Therein All the Days of His Life   Deut. 17:19

Blessed Is He That Readeth   Rev. 1:3

SS1826

Flying high with . . .

DIRECTIONS:
Create this bulletin board using aqua-blue for the background. Use a combination of blue and white paper for the clouds. The kite can be a real kite to give the board a terrific 3-D look. Use yarn and fabric to make a tail. This is a good bulletin board for March and April class projects.

IDEAS:
Use this bulletin board to introduce a study on the miracles connected with WIND.

BONUS ACTIVITY:
On the bulletin board, display Scripture verses about wind that the children find in the Bible. Each time they find a Scripture that mentions WIND, write it on a piece of paper shaped like this:

Attach the Bible verses to the tail of the kite. How long a tail can your class make on the kite?

SCRIPTURE VERSES:
(Miracles connected with wind)
Flood Removed   Gen. 8:1
Locusts Brought and Removed
        Ex. 10:13-19
Red Sea Divided   Ex. 14:21
Quails Provided   Num. 11:31
Rain Brought   I Kings 18:44, 45
Jonah's Ship Tossed   Jonah 1:4
Christ Calms   Matt. 8:26

5

Blooming where I'm planted

DIRECTIONS:
Create this bulletin board using bright, cheerful wrapping paper for the background. Using two main colors, create the blooming flowers. Use green paper for the leaves. Use yellow for the sunrise. You might add Psalm 139:14, "I will praise thee; for I am fearfully and wonderfully made: marvelous are thy works . . ." to emphasize that God does everything well!

IDEAS:
Use this board to develop a creative writing lesson. Have the students write a story about what they would like to be when they become adults. After the stories have been written, encourage the children to illustrate them. Display the stories and pictures on the bulletin board. You might want to follow up with a careers day. Invite some Christian workers to talk to the class about their professions, and about their daily walks with God.

BONUS ACTIVITY:
After the stories and pictures are removed from the bulletin board, seal them in envelopes and date them for twenty years in the future. Have the children take them home and give them to a parent for safekeeping, with the instruction NOT TO BE OPENED FOR TWENTY YEARS.

ALTERNATIVE TITLES AND SCRIPTURE VERSES:
(Walking with God)
Walk in Christ   Col. 2:6
Walk Before God   Gen. 17:1
Walk in Light   I John 1:7
Walk in the Spirit   Gal. 5:16
Walk After the Lord   Hos. 11:10
Walk After the Spirit   Rom. 8:1

6

SS1826

FOR GOD SO LOVED THE WORLD

For God so loved that He gave . . .

DIRECTIONS:
Create this bulletin board using a bright yellow background and brown edging. Use red paper for the heart and trim with real lace or gathered paper. The tomb in the background can be gray and the tree trunk brown. Add green grass and palm fronds. Draw the three crosses after the display is mounted. You may use Romans 5:8 or John 3:16 as the reference for this display.

IDEAS:
Use this board to introduce a Bible study of God's love from creation to the present day.

BONUS ACTIVITY:
Draw a biblical time line on one wall in the classroom. Have students illustrate ways God demonstrated His love for people in the Bible. Place each picture on the appropriate place on the time line.

ALTERNATIVE TITLES AND SCRIPTURE VERSES:
(His Care for His People)

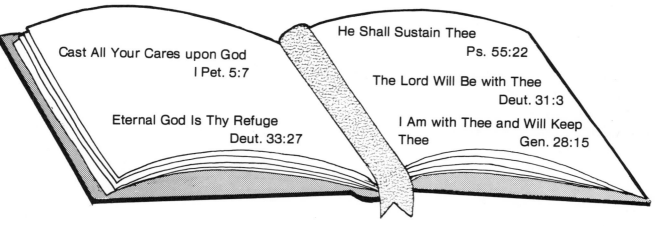

Cast All Your Cares upon God
I Pet. 5:7

Eternal God Is Thy Refuge
Deut. 33:27

He Shall Sustain Thee
Ps. 55:22

The Lord Will Be with Thee
Deut. 31:3

I Am with Thee and Will Keep Thee
Gen. 28:15

7

SS1826

WHAT DOES THE LORD REQUIRE OF THEE?

DIRECTIONS:
Construct this bulletin board using bright pink for the background. Make the bow from strips of paper. Attach the heart to the board, and create a border for it, using hearts or gathered lacy paper.

IDEAS:
Have the children make mobiles of paper hearts and hang from the ceiling. On each heart have the students write a different Scripture verse that tells something about God's love.

BONUS ACTIVITY:
Search the Scriptures for verses that give instructions for following the Lord. Encourage the children to make a list of ten things they can do each day to make their walk with the Lord stronger. Write the instructions on small red hearts and display on the bulletin board.

SCRIPTURE VERSES OF INSTRUCTIONS:
Fear God, and Keep His Commandments   Eccles. 12:13
Fellowship with the Father   I John 1:3
Follow His Steps   I Pet. 2:21
Thou Shalt Love the Lord Thy God   Matt. 22:37
Keep My Commandments   John 14:15

SS1826

**And not
one sparrow
shall fall**

DIRECTIONS:
Create this bulletin board using a pastel yellow or celery-green background. Use tan construction paper for the sparrow, brown for the tree limb and a variety of greens for the leaves. The Scripture thought, found in Matthew 10:29, will help children in times of fear and worry.

IDEAS:
You might use this bulletin board when your class studies birds. Label the different parts of the bird, or display bird reports the children have written on this eye-catching bulletin board. Or you can conduct a Bible quiz that uses birds of the Bible and include this board as part of a learning center.

BONUS ACTIVITY:
Encourage the children to choose an appropriate Bible verse with the theme FEAR NOT. Then have each child create a code by giving each letter of the alphabet a different symbol. Have the students write their Bible verses in code. Exchange papers and let the students decode the messages written by their classmates.

ALTERNATIVE TITLES AND SCRIPTURE VERSES:
(Fear Not)
Be Not Afraid, Only Believe   Mark 5:36
Fear Not, For I Am with Thee   Gen. 26:24
Fear Not, I Am Thy God   Is. 41:10
Fear Not, Little Flock   Luke 12:32
In God I Have Put My Trust   Ps. 56:4

SS1826

My son . . . **forsake not the law of thy mother**

DIRECTIONS:
Create this bulletin board with a pastel pink background. Use red or yellow construction paper for the rose and rosebud. The stem might be made from brown and the leaves from green construction paper. If you are doing the board for Mother's Day, list some of the qualities of a virtuous woman, as found in Proverbs 31:10-31. Try spraying a little perfume to add pizazz to the display.

BONUS ACTIVITY:
Use the rose pattern on this page to decorate personalized stationery for Mother's Day. Children can decorate sheets of paper with a rose and a different Bible phrase about LOVE on each page. Perfume can also be added to the stationery to make this a very special gift for mothers.

ALTERNATIVE TITLES AND SCRIPTURE VERSES:
(Love)
Love Is Kind   I Cor. 13:4
Love Never Faileth   I Cor. 13:8
Knit Together in Love   Col. 2:2
Rooted and Grounded in Love   Eph. 3:17
Let All Things Be Done in Love   I Cor. 16:14
Greatest of These Is Love   I Cor. 13:13
Let Us Love One Another   I John 4:7
See That Ye Love One Another   I Pet. 1:22
Be Kindly Affectioned One to Another   Rom. 12:10
Above All Things Put on Love   Col. 3:14
Love One Another   John 13:34
Love as Brethren   I Pet. 3:8

SS1826

OBEY AND HONOR YOUR PARENTS

DIRECTIONS:
Create this bulletin board using a cheerful printed wrapping-paper design or a pastel background. Use skin-colored construction paper for the parents and children. Use red for the heart. Color in the facial features and hair with felt-tip markers. Use Ephesians 6:1-3 as a Scripture reference. This is a great bulletin board for both Mother's Day and Father's Day.

IDEAS:
Use this display to celebrate families. Two verses that you could use are Genesis 1:27 and Joshua 24:15. Or use Deuteronomy 6:5-9 and add an open Bible to the bulletin board. You may want to have the children draw pictures of their families and display them on the board.

BONUS ACTIVITY:
Take time to have the children create a family tree. You may be surprised at the number of children who do not know the first names of their grandparents and great-grandparents. Encourage the children to take their family trees home to get help filling in the names of ancestors.

SS1826

Winter is past—Spring is here

DIRECTIONS:
Create this bulletin board using a bright yellow background of either construction paper or yellow burlap. The tulips can be a variety of colors. The leaves and grass are made from green paper. Use celery-green for the smiling worm. Add butterflies and ladybugs for extra attraction. If you can find green Easter-basket filling, attach it to the bottom of the board for 3-D grass.

IDEAS:
Use this bulletin board to display names of springtime room helpers.

BONUS ACTIVITY:
First signs of spring always speak to us of hope. Help the children write Haiku poems about hope to celebrate spring! Haiku is a form of Japanese poetry. A Haiku poem is very short, with only seventeen syllables. The first line contains five syllables, the second line contains seven syllables and the third line contains five syllables.

Example: I rejoice in hope,
             Knowing my Lord cares for me
             And is always near.

Have the children study Scripture verses about hope before they begin to write their poems. When the poems are complete, display them on the bulletin board.

ALTERNATIVE TITLES AND SCRIPTURE VERSES:
(Hope)
God of Hope   Rom. 15:13   Hope to the End   I Pet. 1:13
A Living Hope   I Pet. 1:3   Rejoicing in Hope   Rom. 12:12
Abound in Hope   Rom. 15:13

12

SS1826

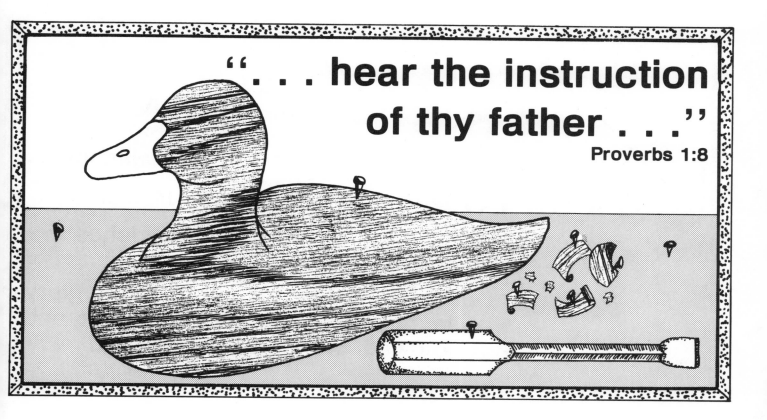

"... hear the instruction of thy father ..."

Proverbs 1:8

DIRECTIONS:
Create this bulletin board with a tan or an orange background. Use brown construction paper or wood-grain Con-Tact paper for the wood duck and shavings. The carving tool can be made from blue or red construction paper with drawn-on details. If you are doing this board for Father's Day, you might use Genesis 18:19, "... he will command his children and his household ... shall keep the way of the Lord ..."

IDEAS:
You may use this bulletin board as a theme display for a wood carving unit in an art class.

BONUS ACTIVITY:
Write acrostic poems for Father's Day. An acrostic poem is a form of Hebrew poetry. Psalm 119 is an example of this kind of poetry. Each of the stanzas begins with a letter from the Hebrew alphabet. Students can write a simple acrostic poem by choosing adjectives that describe their father and that begin with the letters in FATHER. Display all the poems on the board so classroom visitors can enjoy them. Be sure to send the poems home before Father's Day.

Example:
Family
Able
Terrific
Happy
Energetic
Reliable

13

SS1826

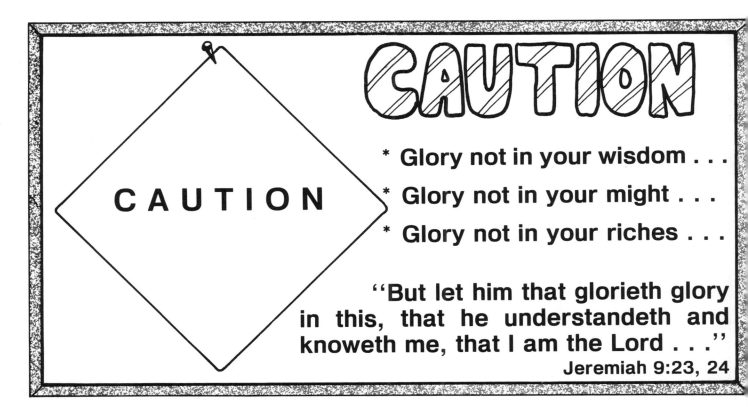

CAUTION

* Glory not in your wisdom . . .
* Glory not in your might . . .
* Glory not in your riches . . .

"But let him that glorieth glory in this, that he understandeth and knoweth me, that I am the Lord . . ."

Jeremiah 9:23, 24

DIRECTIONS:
Create this bulletin board using a bright orange background. Make the caution sign from bright yellow construction paper. Trim with wide black marker.

IDEAS:
Use this display for the beginning of a SAFETY WEEK in your school. Have special signs throughout your room. Invite special guests (firemen, policemen, etc.) to speak to your class on safety. Have the students design safety posters and award some prizes for the best ones. See if you can display the posters in an area store or shopping mall. Take some field trips to different safety facilities in your community (fire station, police station, civil defense post, etc.). You might check into the possibility of some Red Cross training for your students.

BONUS ACTIVITY:
Use the traffic sign patterns on this page and on pages 35, 81, and 84 to create biblical traffic signs. Help the children search the Scriptures for words found on traffic signs. Make the signs into gospel messages by adding biblical phrases.

SS1826

God's word is powerful

DIRECTIONS:
Create this bulletin board using a light blue or celery-green background. Try to find some gold foil wrapping paper or use tinfoil for the sword blade. Use dark green for the grass and leaves. Find other verses that discuss the special characteristics of God's Word. Some of these might include I Peter 1:23-25, Jeremiah 23:29 and Ephesians 6:17.

IDEAS:
Do a study with the students about each of the three noted characteristics of God's Word, as found in Hebrews 4:12. Discuss what it means to be quick, powerful and sharper than a two-edged sword. Then have the children write a brief summary of what this verse means to them.

BONUS ACTIVITY:
In Hebrews 4:12, God's word is compared to a two-edged sword. Have the children write similes about God's word, using examples found in the Bible. A simile is a comparison of two things using the words ''like'' or ''as.'' Make sure the children list the Scripture verses from which they constructed their examples. Display the similes on the bulletin board for all to enjoy.

Example: God's Word is like a seed: it grows where it is planted. Luke 8:11

SCRIPTURE VERSES FOR SIMILIES:
(Word)
The seed is the word.   Luke 8:11
The sword of the Spirit is the word of God.   Eph. 6:17
Thy word is a lamp unto my feet.   Ps. 119:105
Thy word is a light unto my path.   Ps. 119:105
As newborn babes, desire the sincere milk of the word, that
    we may grow thereby.   I Pet. 2:2

SS1826

YOU ARE NOT A MISTAKE

You are not a mistake; you are not simply another ugly toad; you are FEARFULLY and WONDERFULLY made . . .

DIRECTIONS:
Use light blue construction paper for the background. Use either tan or green for the toad. The lily pad could be a contrasting green. Add dark blue for the water. Underline the words ''fearfully'' and ''wonderfully'' for emphasis.

IDEAS:
Look up other verses that discuss God's opinion of each person He has created. Or do an in-depth study of Psalm 139. Take in some commentaries and soon you will see God's loving craftsmanship and creativity.

BONUS ACTIVITY:
Have the children create an ''I Am Wonderfully Made'' collage to celebrate their uniqueness. Let the students cut and paste pictures from magazines that represent important things in their lives. They might spell their names with large letters cut from newspapers or magazines. They may want to add favorite Bible verses to their collages.

ALTERNATIVE TITLES AND SCRIPTURE VERSES:
(God As Creator)
All Things Were Made by Him   John 1:3
God Created Man in His Own Image   Gen. 1:27
God Created Heaven and Earth   Gen. 1:1
We Are His Workmanship   Eph. 2:10
By Him Were All Things Created   Col. 1:16

16

SS1826

Our spring chick says . . .

DIRECTIONS:
Make this bulletin board using light tan or small print wrapping paper for the background. Make the chick using bright yellow construction paper. You may use real straw instead of green grass for the foreground. Display classroom rules, a class project or examples of students' work.

IDEAS:
Use this board to kick off a study of life on the farm, perhaps entitled OLD MAC DONALD'S FARM. For an extended activity, try finding pictures of other barnyard animals to enlarge and display around the room. This could be quite an exciting project. Invite farmers as guests to speak to the children. Or take a field trip to neighboring farms or petting zoos. Have the students choose one farm animal on which to write a report.

BONUS ACTIVITY:
Use this bulletin board to celebrate God's delight in His children. The Bible says God delights in us. Let the children write biblical graffiti on this board, based on the theme of God's delight in each of them.

Example: *God delights in my smile Sarah*   *He loves my violin playing Amy*

ALTERNATIVE TITLES AND SCRIPTURE VERSES:
(God's Delight in Us)
The Lord Delighteth in Thee   Is. 62:4
The Upright Are the Lord's Delight   Prov. 11:20
A Just Weight Is the Lord's Delight   Prov. 11:1
In Whom My Soul Delighteth   Is. 42:1

17

Look what's popping up in our room

DIRECTIONS:

Create the background of this board with light blue construction paper. Make the mushrooms from bright yellow, orange or pink construction paper. Add celery-green grass in the foreground. Add a few brown construction paper pebbles and rocks for that final touch. This board can be used for any theme or subject. It is open to your imagination and creativity. You might use it to list some Christian qualities that you have seen demonstrated in your classroom. Pass out mushroom-shaped awards to children who demonstrate these qualities.

IDEAS:

Since heavy spring rains usually lead to the growth of mushrooms, this might be a good time to teach about mushrooms in your science class. Research the topic together as a class and then see if you can take a field trip to hunt for mushrooms. As a culminating activity, bring in foods that use mushrooms as ingredients. Examples: pizza, casseroles and breaded mushrooms.

BONUS ACTIVITY:

Create an original and unique seed catalog. Encourage each child to think up a new and original plant. It might be a blooming flower, a fruit tree or a brand new vegetable that no one has ever tasted. Next have the students draw pictures of the plant, describe its unique qualities and give it a name. Then compile all the pages into a class catalog of new and original plants.

ALTERNATIVE TITLES AND SCRIPTURE VERSES:
(Growth)
That Ye May Grow Thereby   I Pet. 2:2
Grow in Grace   II Pet. 3:18
Grow Up into Him in All Things   Eph. 4:15

God's breath of new life . . .

SPRING

DIRECTIONS:
Let your creativity explode when you do this bulletin board. Start with a bright yellow background. Use generous spring colors for the wording, the flower and the butterfly. You might let the class put the finishing touches on this board.

IDEAS:
Welcome spring with a bulletin board contest. Have individual classrooms create their own bulletin boards with a spring theme. Then have the art teacher be the final judge. Award some special prizes such as candy, award certificates, extra recess or a class party to the winners. This project will be a real face-lift for the entire school or church. You may want to plan an open house around the contest. Invite parents to tour the rooms and see all the displays.

BONUS ACTIVITY:
Use the butterfly and flower theme on this board to create invitations to the open house. Let the children make posters announcing the bulletin board contest. You may also want the children to make the awards for the winners.

ALTERNATIVE TITLES AND SCRIPTURE VERSES:
(Joy)
Rejoice!   I Pet. 4:13
Shout for Joy   Ps. 35:27
Rejoice Evermore   I Thess. 5:16
Rejoice in the Lord   Phil. 4:4
Be Glad in the Lord   Ps. 32:11

19

 SS1826

And Jesus entered triumphantly

"Hosanna!" "Hosanna!"

DIRECTIONS:
Create this bulletin board using light green for the background. Mount dark green leaves or real palm branches in the upper righthand corner. Use gray or brown for the building outlines. Add a scriptural prophesy of the Messiah's triumphal entry into Jerusalem.

IDEAS:
Look up the New Testament verses that share insight into the fulfillment of this prophecy. They include Matthew 21:1-9, Mark 11:1-10, Luke 19:29-38 and John 12:12-19.

BONUS ACTIVITY:
Have a class contest to see who can list the most Old Testament prophecies fulfilled by Jesus. Students should list the Old Testament prophecy (book, chapter and verse) and then list the Scripture in the New Testament that fulfilled the prophecy.

ALTERNATIVE TITLES AND SCRIPTURE VERSES:
(Rejoice)

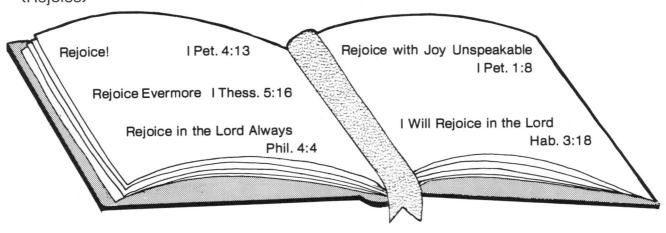

Rejoice!   I Pet. 4:13

Rejoice Evermore I Thess. 5:16

Rejoice in the Lord Always
                Phil. 4:4

Rejoice with Joy Unspeakable
                I Pet. 1:8

I Will Rejoice in the Lord
                Hab. 3:18

EASTER MEANS FORGIVENESS

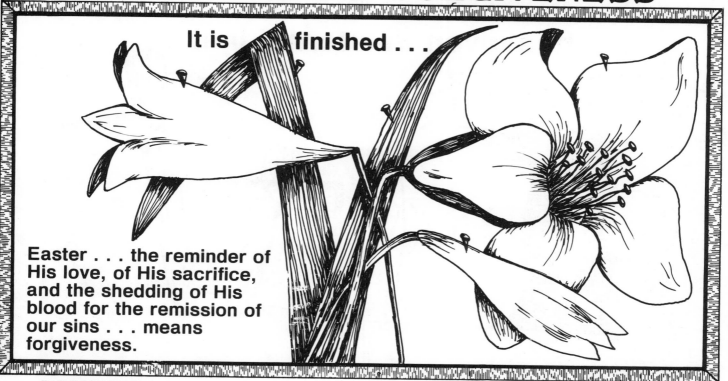

It is finished . . .

Easter . . . the reminder of His love, of His sacrifice, and the shedding of His blood for the remission of our sins . . . means forgiveness.

DIRECTIONS:
Make this bulletin board very simple. Use a light color for the background. The Easter lily should be made from white paper and the slender leaf made from green paper. The lettering can be done in red.

IDEAS:
Have each child draw a picture portraying some part of the Easter story. Put the pictures in sequential order and display them on the bulletin board.

BONUS ACTIVITY:
Help bring this story to life for your students by putting them ''in the picture.'' Have them create a newspaper headline and story or an eyewitness TV report about the Resurrection of Jesus. The article should be written as if the child is a reporter covering the story as it happened.

ALTERNATIVE TITLES AND SCRIPTURE VERSES:
(Resurrection of Jesus)

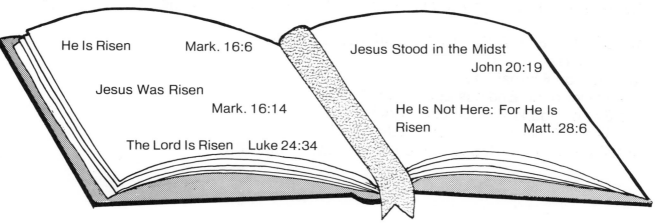

He Is Risen   Mark. 16:6

Jesus Was Risen
                Mark. 16:14

The Lord Is Risen   Luke 24:34

Jesus Stood in the Midst
                John 20:19

He Is Not Here: For He Is
Risen   Matt. 28:6

21

SS1826

God has given us eternal life!

DIRECTIONS:
Create this bulletin board using a medium blue background. Use green for the grass. Enlarge the tomb and crosses used on page 7, using gray and brown construction paper. Use a felt-tip marker to do the shading and details. You can have the students write or draw pictures of what Easter means to them. Encourage them to include how Christ showed His love for each of them. Use I John 5:11-13 as the Scripture reference for this board.

IDEAS:
Do a study of Christian gospel songs that develop this same theme. Bring in some records to play and have the children memorize some of the songs.

BONUS ACTIVITY:
Just for fun, have the children design jackets for Christian record albums. Make sure the record jackets highlight the Scripture messages of the songs.

ALTERNATIVE TITLES AND SCRIPTURE VERSES:
(Eternal Life)
Lay Hold on Eternal Life   I Tim. 6:12
The Power of an Endless Life   Heb. 7:16
The Gift of God Is Eternal Life   Rom. 6:23
This Is the Promise . . . Eternal Life   I John 2:25
I Shall Dwell in the House of the Lord for Ever   Ps. 23:6

22

SUMMER

SS1826

Mount up
with wings as
eagles

DIRECTIONS:
Create this board using a bright blue background. Enlarge the head of the eagle so it is the focal point. Using paper with curved edges, create the scroll and attach it to the board. You may use the entire passage Isaiah 40:28-31, or just a few phrases, depending on the ages of the students and where the board is to be displayed. Underline the words that you wish to highlight. Challenge your students to excel in work habits this school year. Remind them to keep the Lord Jesus Christ first and to draw upon Him for the strength they need each day.

IDEAS:
You might use this display when you teach United States history. Use the eagle and a flag of the United States, as well as other symbols of our country, to embellish your classroom. You may use II Chronicles 7:14 as your theme for the display. This will be a good bulletin board to display around the Fourth of July.

BONUS ACTIVITY:
Discuss the United States flag, and then have the children design their own flags. They should use colors and symbols that represent their faith and love of God. Completed flags may be displayed on and around the board.

ALTERNATIVE TITLES AND SCRIPTURE VERSES:
(Waiting For God)
Wait Ye upon Me   Zeph. 3:8
Wait on the Lord   Prov. 20:22
Wait Patiently for Him   Ps. 37:7
Wait on Thy God Continually   Hos. 12:6
I Wait for the Lord   Ps. 130:5
We Have Waited for Him   Is. 25:9

24

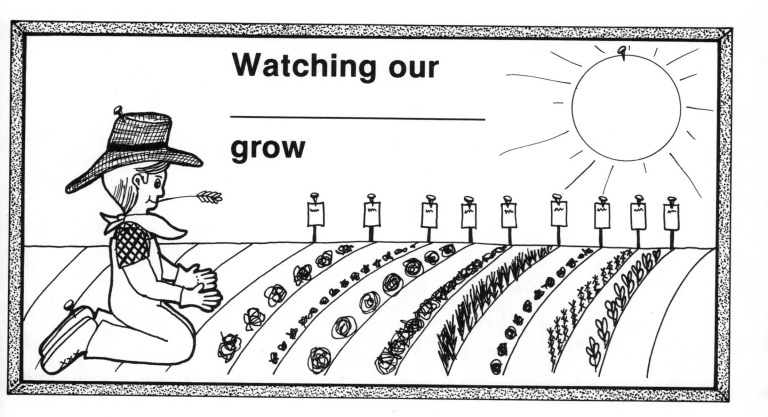

Watching our

grow

DIRECTIONS:
Create this bulletin board by first doing the background in light blue. The foreground can then be done in different shades of brown, tan, and other earth tones. If possible, use real seed packages to identify the rows of plants. Make the farmer with blue bib overalls, a yellow straw hat, red handkerchief and brown shoes. Use a real handkerchief if possible. Make plants from green construction paper.

IDEAS:
You may choose to use this bulletin board when you study plants or agriculture. Use Ephesians 4:15, a Scripture passage that demonstrates the idea of growing up into Him in all things.

BONUS ACTIVITY:
Challenge the children to choose a Bible verse about HARVEST or GROWTH and create a crossword puzzle or a word-search puzzle. Exchange papers and let classmates solve each others' puzzles.

ALTERNATIVE TITLES AND SCRIPTURE VERSES:
(Harvest)
The Fields . . . White Already to Harvest
    John 4:35
The Harvest Is Ripe   Joel 3:13
The Harvest Is the End of the World   Matt. 13:39
The Harvest Is Past, the Summer Is Ended
    Jer. 8:20

SS1826

Waves of great work

DIRECTIONS:
Create this bulletin board with a light blue background, dark blue water and brown pier posts. The bird can be a white seagull. Use a felt-tip marker to draw on the spraying water as it hits the pier posts. You might subtitle this board "Our Best for Our Lord," and use it to display students' work.

IDEAS:
Use this bulletin board to do a study of the ocean. Or use it to display ocean-theme art projects that the children complete.

BONUS ACTIVITY:
All jobs are important and should be done well. Emphasize the importance of all occupations and reinforce Bible stories by having your students write want ads based on biblical stories.

ALTERNATIVE TITLES AND SCRIPTURE VERSES:
(Workmanship)

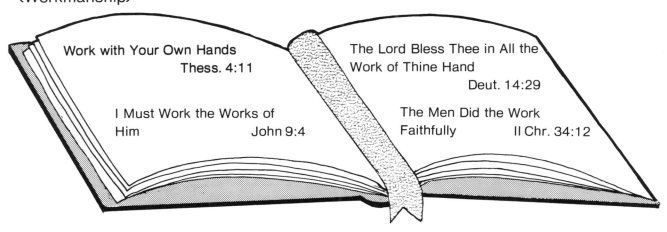

Work with Your Own Hands
Thess. 4:11

I Must Work the Works of
Him   John 9:4

The Lord Bless Thee in All the
Work of Thine Hand
Deut. 14:29

The Men Did the Work
Faithfully   II Chr. 34:12

I AM THE VINE

"I am the vine,
ye are the
branches . . ."
John 15:5

DIRECTIONS:
Bring John 15:5 to life with this attention-getting board. Use an off-white background and purple and violet grapes. Use brown construction paper for the stem and add green leaves. Cut some brown construction paper spirals for the vines. On the grapes you might choose to write principles that produce a fruitful life.

IDEAS:
Use this bulletin board as a display for a team competition. You can title it "Bunching Together to Win." In the corner you can display current scores or the rules of the competition.

BONUS ACTIVITY:
Take this opportunity to have the children do a self-evaluation of their efforts. Begin by having them create their own report card and grade themselves in all areas. Then ask them to list the areas in which they need to be more diligent. Culminate this self-evaluation lesson by having the children write plans for self-improvement in one area.

ALTERNATIVE TITLES AND SCRIPTURE VERSES:
(Diligence)
Be Not Slothful in Business   Rom. 12:11
Study to Be Quiet   I Thess. 4:11
Do It with Thy Might   Eccles. 9:10
He Did It with All His Heart   II Chr. 31:21
Be Diligent That Ye May Be Found of Him   II Pet. 3:14

Shining Star Publications, Copyright © 1987, A division of Good Apple, Inc.

SS1826

ONE NATION UNDER GOD

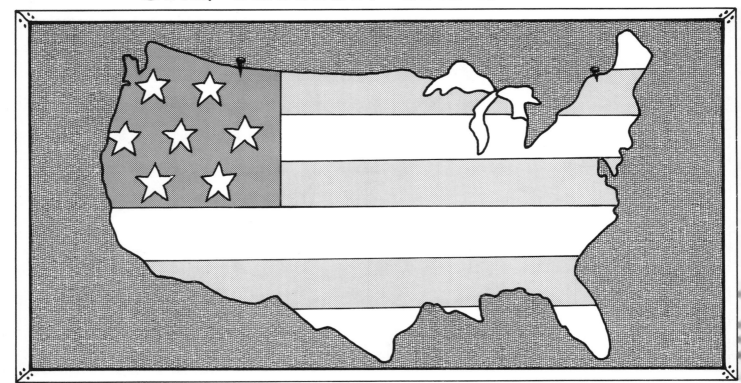

DIRECTIONS:
Create this bulletin board using light blue construction paper or fabric. Decorate an outline of the United States to resemble our country's flag. Use red and white for the stripes and dark blue with white stars at the top left-hand corner. Around the outside, display pictures of different churches, types of worship services, etc.

IDEAS:
Use this bulletin board to teach facts about the United States. Fill the outline with different symbols of the U.S.A. You could label different cities, parks, natural land features, etc.

BONUS ACTIVITY:
Use the map on this bulletin board to challenge the class to write letters and create goodwill. Begin by having the children write letters to people in every state in the United States. As the children receive answers to their letters, attach the cancelled stamps in the appropriate spots on the map. Can your class collect cancelled stamps from all fifty states? If they enjoy this project, put up a world map and see if they can obtain cancelled stamps from every country in the world.

ALTERNATIVE TITLES AND SCRIPTURE VERSES:
(Brotherliness)
Let Brotherly Love Continue   Heb. 13:1
Add to Your Godliness Brotherly Kindness   II Pet. 1:7
Be Kindly Affectioned One to Another with Brotherly
     Love   Rom. 12:10

"...keep thyself pure."
I Timothy 5:22

DIRECTIONS:
Create this bulletin board using light tan for the background to symbolize the desert sand. Use brown and black to create the scorpion. Use green or darker brown for the cactus and yellow for the sun. Highlight the stinger on the scorpion's tail. You might want to use I Timothy 5:22 for the Scripture reference.

IDEAS:
Use this bulletin board when you study plant and animal life of the desert. Add additional plants and animals that you will be discussing in your unit study. Or display student papers on desert subjects.

BONUS ACTIVITY:
Encourage each child to create a biblical bumper sticker. The sticker should reflect an important Christian message about clean living.

ALTERNATIVE TITLES AND SCRIPTURE VERSES:
(Clean Living)

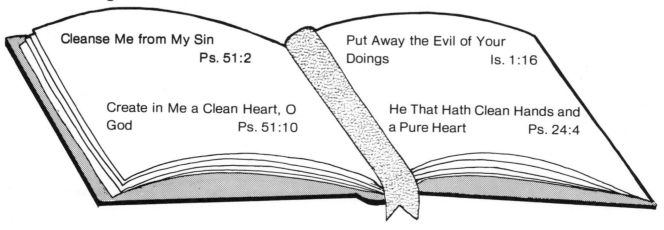

Cleanse Me from My Sin
Ps. 51:2

Put Away the Evil of Your Doings
Is. 1:16

Create in Me a Clean Heart, O God
Ps. 51:10

He That Hath Clean Hands and a Pure Heart
Ps. 24:4

SS1826

If sinners entice thee . . .

DIRECTIONS:
Create this bulletin board using browns, tans, greens and other earth tones. Make the snake from complementary colors. Staple or pin dried leaves and plant stems to the board to add to the realism. Draw a rattler on the end of the snake's tail with a felt-tip marker. Make the trees and frog from green construction paper. The reference for this board could be Proverbs 1:10-19.

IDEAS:
Use this board when you teach a lesson about snakes or other interesting animals.

BONUS ACTIVITY:
Take a Scripture safari through the Bible to reinforce this bulletin board theme. The children are to search for the names of animals mentioned in the Bible. They should list the name of the animal and the appropriate Scripture verse. You may want to make this a class competition to see who can find the most animals in a given time. Give one point for every animal found and a bonus of three points for any animals found that were not found by anyone else.

ALTERNATIVE TITLES AND SCRIPTURE VERSES:
(Sin)
All Have Sinned   Rom. 3:23
Christ Came to Save Sinners   I Tim. 1:15
God Taketh Away the Sin of the World
     John 1:29
Cleanseth Us from All Sin   I John 1:7

" . . . let patience have her perfect work . . ."

James 1:4

DIRECTIONS:
Create this bulletin board with a light tan background. The snail can be made from either bright orange or yellow paper. Add colored flowers and green leaves, grass and foreground. Use James 1:4 as a Scripture verse for this display. This is an excellent springboard for a discussion on patience. You may want to define patience on the board. (The ability to bear trials without complaining.)

IDEAS:
Use this display to bring in summer. Add some flowers, frogs, and other summer creatures. The snail might be a good graphic to be used on a work sheet about patience.

BONUS ACTIVITY:
Pantomiming takes a great amount of patience. Give your children the opportunity to practice PATIENCE by performing biblical pantomimes. The first classmate to guess the story being pantomimed gets to be next to share his/her biblical pantomime.

ALTERNATIVE TITLES AND SCRIPTURE VERSES:
(Patience)
Be Patient in Tribulation   Rom. 12:12
Be Patient Toward All Men   I Thess. 5:14
Wait Patiently for Him   Ps. 37:7
Be Patient   James 5:7
Let Us Run with Patience the Race Set Before Us
    Heb. 12:1

SS1826

LET YOUR LIGHT SHINE

"Let your light so shine before men . . ."

Matt. 5:16

DIRECTIONS:
Create this eye-catching bulletin board using a bright yellow background. Use brown for the bushel basket and tree stump. The candle may be orange or blue with a red and yellow flame. The candleholder may be any color you choose. The foreground should be green. Use a felt-tip marker to add the lines to make the candle appear to be shining brightly. Matthew 5:14-16 are good verses for this display.

IDEAS:
Use this display, but add different verses that discuss the quality of light. Ephesians 5:8 and I John 1:5 are two possibilities. This is a good bulletin board for a missionary conference or a missionary visiting day at your school.

BONUS ACTIVITY:
A rebus message is a story that has pictures replacing words or word parts. For example:

👁 L-arm-r   3-re   💡

Have your students choose their favorite Bible verse about LIGHT and write it as a rebus message. The more pictures used to replace words the better!

ALTERNATIVE TITLES AND SCRIPTURE VERSES:
(Light)
The Lord Is My Light   Ps. 27:1
I Am the Light of the World   John 8:12
Ye Are Children of Light   I Thess. 5:5
Ye Are the Light of the World   Matt. 5:14
God Is Light   I John 1:5

Shining Star Publications, Copyright © 1987, A division of Good Apple, Inc.   SS1826

A BROKEN SPIRIT DRIETH THE BONES

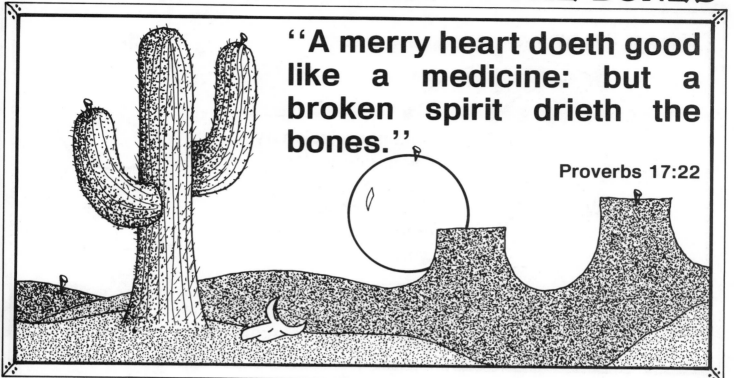

"A merry heart doeth good like a medicine: but a broken spirit drieth the bones."

Proverbs 17:22

DIRECTIONS:
Create this bulletin board using bright orange for the background, brown and tan for the hills and foreground, yellow for the sun and green for the cactus. The skull should be white. The Scripture reference for this display is found in Proverbs 17:22.

IDEAS:
Contrast the cactus in this display to the tree that is planted by the rivers of water (Psalm 1:3).

BONUS ACTIVITY:
"A merry heart doeth good like medicine." If this is true, we must remember to have a good sense of humor with our children. For a light-hearted Bible lesson, have your students write biblical puns. A pun is defined as a play on words which sound the same but have different meanings, or on different applications of a word, producing a witty effect. Have the children choose their favorite Bible story and write a pun about it. Example: When David met Goliath, he had a GIANT problem.

ALTERNATIVE TITLES AND SCRIPTURE VERSES:
(Happiness)

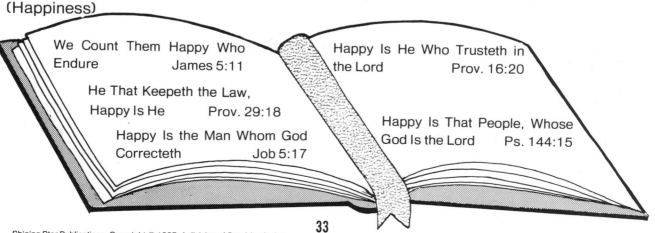

We Count Them Happy Who Endure   James 5:11

He That Keepeth the Law, Happy Is He   Prov. 29:18

Happy Is the Man Whom God Correcteth   Job 5:17

Happy Is He Who Trusteth in the Lord   Prov. 16:20

Happy Is That People, Whose God Is the Lord   Ps. 144:15

SS1826

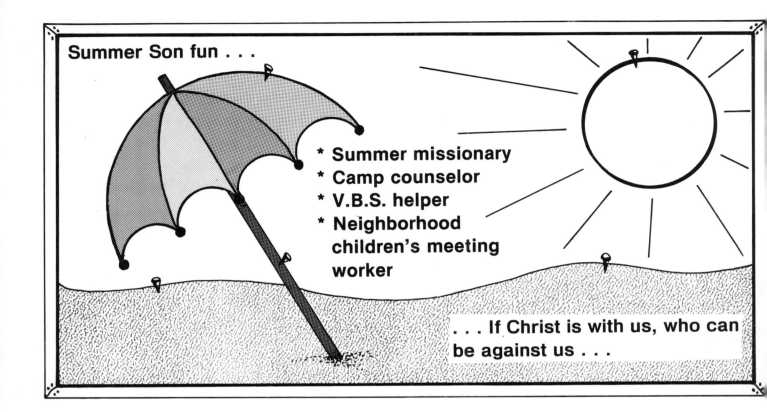

Summer Son fun . . .

* **Summer missionary**
* **Camp counselor**
* **V.B.S. helper**
* **Neighborhood children's meeting worker**

. . . If Christ is with us, who can be against us . . .

DIRECTIONS:
Create this bulletin board with a bright yellow background. Draw the sun on the yellow background with a felt-tip marker. The beach should be tan construction paper. You may want to make the umbrella with a rainbow of colors for a really eye-catching display.

IDEAS:
Have each child write out his personal goals for the summer and place them on a construction paper beach ball. Attach the ''beach balls'' on the board for all to share. Then later in the summer, send those goals to the children as a special reminder.

BONUS ACTIVITY:
Have each child make three calendars with writing space for each day of the summer months. Daily goals set can be listed. For example: say my prayers; read one Bible verse; do a good deed. Each day that a goal is met the child can color in that square or make a special note of his/her accomplishment on the calendar. This aid will help children establish a daily schedule for building his/her faith.

ALTERNATIVE TITLES AND SCRIPTURE VERSES:
(Established)
Established with Grace   Heb. 13:9
Established in Faith   Acts 16:5
Established in Righteousness   Is. 54:14
Established in Every Good Word and Work   II Thess. 2:17,
Established, Rooted and Built Up in Christ   Col. 2:7

SS1826

DIRECTIONS:
This bulletin board can be very effective if kept simple. Use white for the background and red for the stop sign. Add a brown trunk, green leaves and green grass. Add the lines of the sidewalk with felt-tip marker. You may want to list several Scripture verses that tell of things that God commands us to STOP doing. Depending on the goals you have, list the appropriate Scripture or message on the bulletin board.

IDEAS:
Highlight Bible stories of how God stopped some things. Name stories and list appropriate Bible verses on the bulletin board. Examples: the Red Sea parting; mouths of lions being closed; imprisonment of His Disciples; the rain and the stormy sea.

BONUS ACTIVITY:
Have students draw biblical cartoons to culminate the lesson on things God stopped. Begin by brainstorming a list of fifteen or twenty Bible stories about things that were stopped by God. Then have each child choose his favorite story and depict it in a cartoon strip. Display these Bible cartoon strips on the bulletin board.

ALTERNATIVE TITLES AND SCRIPTURE VERSES:
(God's Infinite Power)
With God All Things Are Possible   Matt. 19:26
Is Anything Too Hard for the Lord?   Gen. 18:14
With God Nothing Shall Be Impossible   Luke 1:37
All Power Is Given unto Me in Heaven   Matt. 28:18

SS1826

Buzzzzzzzing by with . . .

DIRECTIONS:
Make this bulletin board with a light blue background. The bee may be yellow and black with white wings. Use gold or beige honeycomb sections for added attraction.

IDEAS:
This board can be used to highlight a learning center on insects. If you are doing a study of bees in your classroom, add a large beehive and display the bee reports on this board.

BONUS ACTIVITY:
Bees are busy filling their combs with honey each day. With what are we busily filling our daily lives? The Bible has specific instructions about how to fill our days. After studying the Scripture verses below, have the children choose one verse and make a slogan from it. Next have the children use their slogans to create buttons to wear to tell others of their faith.

EXAMPLE:

SCRIPTURE VERSES:
Filled with Joy.   II Tim. 1:4
Filled with Wisdom.   Luke 2:40
Filled with Comfort.   II Cor. 7:4
Filled with Knowledge.   Rom. 15:14
Filled with Righteousness.   Matt. 5:6
Filled with the Holy Ghost.   Acts 4:8
Filled with the Fullness of God.   Eph. 3:19

36

KEEP YOUR LIFE CLEAN DAILY

**Keep your life clean daily . . .
For you are bought with a price:
Therefore glorify God in your
body and spirit . . .**

DIRECTIONS:
Use a light orange background for this bulletin board. Make the pail from tan or gray paper. Use brown for the mop handle and white for the mop head. Draw in the details of the mop with felt-tip marker. You might want to display Ephesians 4:1 on this board.

IDEAS:
This display could be used as a springboard for a career day in your classroom. Every job, no matter what type, should be performed to glorify God.

BONUS ACTIVITY:
To emphasize the many different occupations mentioned in the Bible, have the children write biblical resumes. Students should choose a favorite biblical character and then write a resume for that person's occupation.

ALTERNATIVE TITLES AND SCRIPTURE VERSES:
(Glorifying God)

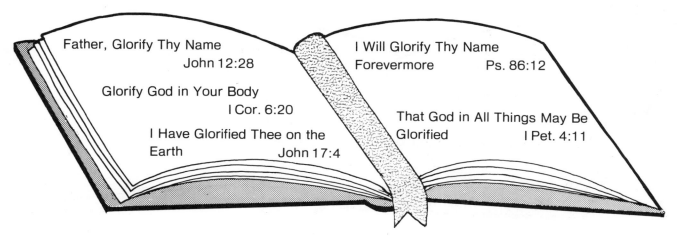

Father, Glorify Thy Name
John 12:28

Glorify God in Your Body
I Cor. 6:20

I Have Glorified Thee on the
Earth
John 17:4

I Will Glorify Thy Name
Forevermore
Ps. 86:12

That God in All Things May Be
Glorified
I Pet. 4:11

SS1826

Moving right along . . .

DIRECTIONS:
The background for this board should be a bright small print wrapping paper. Use bright green construction paper for the grasshopper. Make the details of the grasshopper with a felt-tip marker.

IDEAS:
This board could also be used to display the school calendar, the church calendar or to advertise upcoming events.

BONUS ACTIVITY:
Practice handwriting by having the children write their favorite Bible verses about GOOD WORKS. Hang the best papers on the bulletin board for everyone to admire.

ALTERNATIVE TITLES AND SCRIPTURE VERSES:
(Good Works)

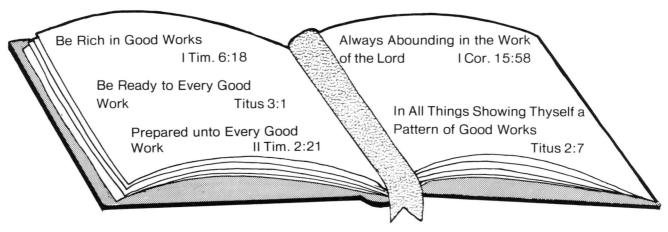

Be Rich in Good Works
I Tim. 6:18

Always Abounding in the Work of the Lord
I Cor. 15:58

Be Ready to Every Good Work
Titus 3:1

Prepared unto Every Good Work
II Tim. 2:21

In All Things Showing Thyself a Pattern of Good Works
Titus 2:7

SS1826

DON'T STRIKE OUT

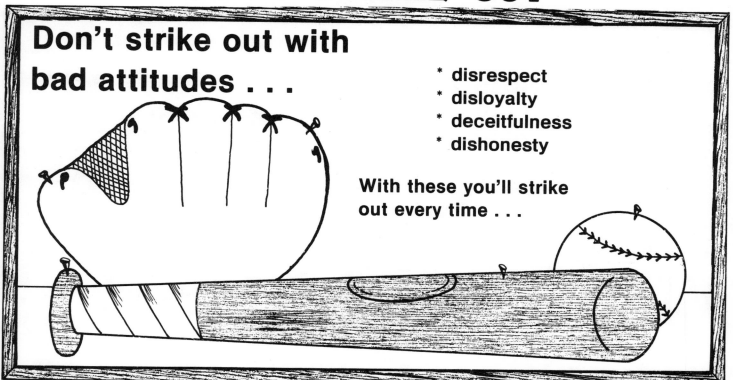

Don't strike out with bad attitudes . . .

* disrespect
* disloyalty
* deceitfulness
* dishonesty

With these you'll strike out every time . . .

DIRECTIONS:
Make the background of this bulletin board celery-green. The bat should be tan and the ball white construction paper. You may want to list other bad attitudes in addition to the ones suggested.

IDEAS:
Use the bulletin board to announce upcoming sports events or team competitions.

BONUS ACTIVITY:
Reinforce positive attitudes by having your students create T-shirt designs with good attitude slogans. Draw the designs on paper T-shirts.
Example: Come Join God's Team!

ALTERNATIVE TITLES AND SCRIPTURE VERSES:
(Delight)
I Delight in the Law of God   Rom. 7:22
I Delight to Do Thy Will   Ps. 40:8
His Delight is in the Law of the Lord   Ps. 1:2
Delight Thyself Also in the Lord   Ps. 37:4

Shining Star Publications, Copyright © 1987, A division of Good Apple, Inc.

SS1826

You'll be nuts about . . .

DIRECTIONS:
Create this bulletin board with an orange background. Make the peanut/walnut from tan construction paper. Add the details with a felt-tip marker.

IDEAS:
This bulletin board could be used to introduce George Washington Carver, who developed the peanut. He displayed tremendous character and genius. Study other Christian people who helped make our country great.

BONUS ACTIVITY:
Challenge your students to make a book jacket for their favorite book of the Bible. The pictures on the jacket should depict important facts contained in that book, or should clearly illustrate the life of a Bible hero.

ALTERNATIVE TITLES AND SCRIPTURE VERSES:
(Sowing and Reaping)
Forgive, and Ye Shall Be Forgiven   Luke 6:37
Give and It Shall Be Given unto You   Luke 6:38
Whatsoever a Man Soweth, That Shall He Also Reap
    Gal. 6:7
He Which Soweth Bountifully Shall Reap Also Bountifully
    II Cor. 9:6

                    SS1826

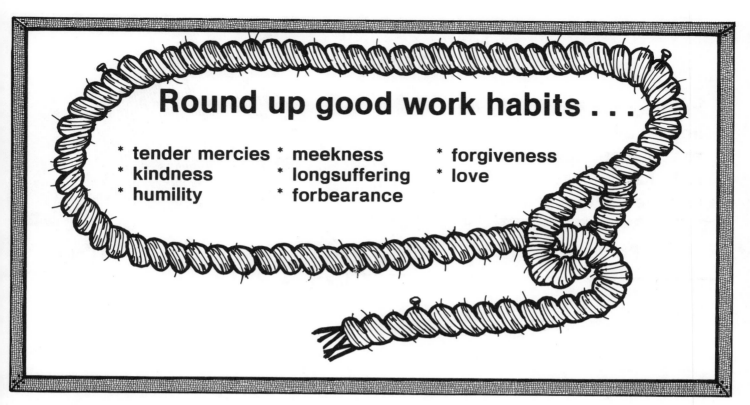

Round up good work habits . . .

* tender mercies * meekness   * forgiveness
* kindness   * longsuffering * love
* humility   * forbearance

DIRECTIONS:
Make the background of this board any color you choose. Use a real piece of rope or make one from tan construction paper. Make the list of good habits large enough so it can be easily read. Add additional western symbols or pictures of cowboys. You may use the boot pictured on page 48.

IDEAS:
You may use this board as your yearly job board for classroom chores. Title it "Responsibility Roundup." List the jobs on pieces of paper cut in appropriate shapes. Attach classroom job descriptions to the board and put a nail beside each of the jobs. Then you can change names next to each job every week.

BONUS ACTIVITY:
Stimulate Bible research by challenging your students to make a list of Bible characters and their occupations. Play a matching game to get them started. On the chalkboard, list the nine biblical characters and the nine occupations found below. The children must match the Bible hero with his/her occupation. Then challenge them to find other heroes and list their occupations too. Who can make the longest list? Would this be a good team game?

Joshua, Dorcas, Nimrod, Paul, Nehemiah, David, Peter, Matthew and Luke
doctor, tax collector, fisherman, shepherd, cup-bearer, tentmaker, hunter, seamstress and soldier

ALTERNATIVE TITLES AND SCRIPTURE VERSES:
(Work)
The Work Which Thou Gavest Me
                              John 17:4

Study to Be Quiet and to Work with Your Own Hands
                              I Thess. 4:11

41

SS1826

Flee temptation

"Ponder the path of thy feet, and let all thy ways be established. Turn not to the right hand nor to the left: remove thy foot from evil."

Proverbs 4:26,27

DIRECTIONS:
Use dark brown paper for the baseboard and a light celery-green for the wall. Or use real wallpaper for the wall. The mouse should be tan and the trap can be brown construction paper. Don't forget to put a large piece of orange cheese on the mousetrap.

IDEAS:
Look up Bible verses that discuss temptation. Use these verses for a class discussion. As a class, brainstorm a list of weapons we can use to gain victory over temptation. Ephesians 6:10-17 lists some of the armor we can use.

BONUS ACTIVITY:
Visualizing something sometimes helps us make it come true. Help your students overcome a bad habit or temptation by encouraging them to draw and color a picture of themselves overcoming it. Example: A child who overeats might draw a picture of himself saying NO to a sweet dessert. A child who watches too much television might draw a picture of herself reading a book. Encourage the children to share and talk about what they have drawn. (This should be voluntary, of course.) Tell the children to keep their pictures at home and to put a star on the back every time they exert willpower to break the bad habit.

ALTERNATIVE TITLES AND SCRIPTURE VERSES:
(Temptation)
Lead Us Not into Temptation   Matt. 6:13
Pray That Ye Enter Not into Temptation   Matt. 26:41
With God Nothing Shall Be Impossible   Luke 1:37
Blessed Is the Man That Endureth Temptation   James 1:12
God Will Not Suffer You to Be Tempted Above That Ye Are
     Able   I Cor. 10:13

42

                    SS1826

FALL

43

Giving thanks always

DIRECTIONS:
Create this bulletin board using brown construction paper for the cornucopia and for the bushel basket. Add different colored fruit resting on green leaves. The wheat can either be real or made from brown or yellow construction paper. Burnt orange burlap or orange construction paper would be ideal for the background. Use this bulletin board to express the commandment of Ephesians 5:20, "Giving thanks always for all things unto God and the Father in the name of our Lord Jesus Christ." You might also use Psalm 140:13.

IDEAS:
Do a study of Scripture passages that discuss the theme of giving thanks. Psalms might be a good place to start. Consider doing a thanksgiving offering for one of your church's special missionaries or staff members. This could be done either as a class or as an entire school. If you have some missionaries on furlough attending your school, you might consider a food offering that would be brought in by the students.

BONUS ACTIVITY:
Have your students take time to think about someone who helps them in some special way. Then encourage the children to write a thank-you note to this person. This could be the school crossing guard, a neighbor who takes time to talk to them or any other person who gives time and effort to children. The children may want to design awards to be given to people for kind deeds they have done.

ALTERNATIVE TITLES AND SCRIPTURE VERSES:
(Thanksgiving)
Be Ye Thankful   Col. 3:15
In Every Thing Give Thanks   I Thess. 5:18
Abounding with Thanksgiving   Col. 2:7
Giving Thanks Always for All Things   Eph. 5:20

                    SS1826

Harvest of the Lord's goodness

DIRECTIONS:
Create this bulletin board using red for the barn, blue or tan for the silo, and different shades of brown and gray for the landscape. Use light blue for the background and yellow for the sun and the path leading to the barn. Finally, add golden stacks of hay scattered on the hillsides. Use this bulletin board to remind the children of the Lord's goodness during this season of the year. There are many Scripture references that you could include in your instruction that express our responsibility to give thanks unto the Lord. You might use Psalm 24:1 as a Scripture passage.

IDEAS:
Do a study on the history of agriculture, comparing yesterday's farming methods with today's. God not only has blessed us with food, but also has given us the ability to improve the ways men harvest the Lord's goodness. You might have students illustrate examples of different ways of farming and draw pictures of farm machinery to display around the central bulletin board.

BONUS ACTIVITY:
You can make God's goodness more concrete to your students by having them write poetry. Each child begins by thinking of an object that he or she is very thankful for. Then the child writes a two-line rhyming poem that tells about this object. Write the poem in the shape of the object. Display the concrete poems on the path of this bulletin board.

Example: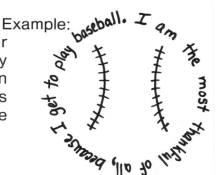

ALTERNATIVE TITLES AND SCRIPTURE VERSES:
(God's Goodness)

How Great Is His Goodness Zech. 9:17	O Taste and See That the Lord Is Good
For He Is Good Ps. 107:1	Ps. 34:8
The Goodness of God Endureth	O How Great Is Thy Goodness Ps. 31:19
Continually Ps. 52:1	

45

Shining Star Publications, Copyright © 1987, A division of Good Apple, Inc.   SS1826

THE HARVEST IS PLENTEOUS

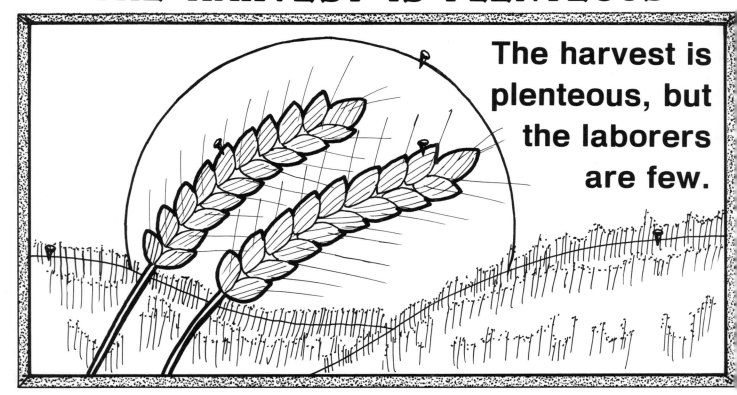

The harvest is plenteous, but the laborers are few.

DIRECTIONS:
Create this bulletin board with a light blue background. The sun should be bright yellow, and the wheat brown. The reference for this bulletin board is found in Matthew 9:37, 38. This would be an excellent display to use during a missionary's visit.

IDEAS:
Use this bulletin board around Thanksgiving time and add several other typical items from the farmer's harvest.

BONUS ACTIVITY:
Share the story of Naomi and Ruth, two poor women who came to Bethlehem during barley harvest time. Then have students pretend they are gleaners in Boaz' field. Have each student write a conversation that might have taken place between Ruth and another gleaner. Let some of the students dramatize their stories. Post the conversations on the board for everyone to read and enjoy.

ALTERNATIVE TITLES AND SCRIPTURE VERSES:
(God as Provider)

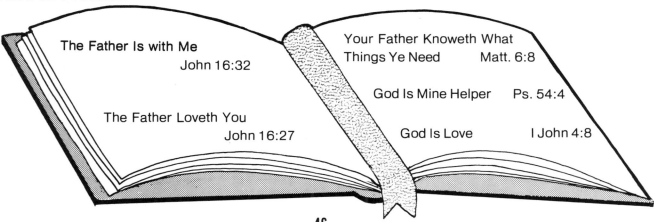

The Father Is with Me
John 16:32

The Father Loveth You
John 16:27

Your Father Knoweth What Things Ye Need   Matt. 6:8

God Is Mine Helper   Ps. 54:4

God Is Love   I John 4:8

The Bible—God's treasure

DIRECTIONS:
Create this bulletin board using white or light blue for the background. The treasure chest can be made from brown construction paper, with gold foil or yellow paper used for the gold pieces. Use tan for the beach. You might also include Psalm 119:18 written on the pages of the Bible: "Open thou mine eyes, that I may behold wondrous things out of thy law."

IDEAS:
Use this display to teach important passages and truths about God's Word. Some passages that come to mind are Psalm 19:7-10 and Psalm 119. Let your creativity develop this display into one of your best yet!

BONUS ACTIVITY:
Fill the treasure chest on this bulletin board with "heavenly riches." Have the children make a list of the things in their lives that make them truly rich in the Lord. Examples: faith, prayer, Christian parents. Then cut coin shapes from gold construction paper and write each "treasure" on a coin. Have the children attach their own coins to the board.

ALTERNATIVE TITLES AND SCRIPTURE VERSES:
(Riches)
The Riches of His Grace   Eph. 2:7
The Riches of His Glory   Rom. 9:23
The Riches of God's Goodness   Rom. 2:4
The Riches of Full Assurance   Col. 2:2
The Unsearchable Riches of Christ   Eph. 3:8
The Riches of the Wisdom of God   Rom. 11:33
The Riches of the Glory of His Inheritance   Eph. 1:18

Shining Star Publications, Copyright © 1987, A division of Good Apple, Inc.   SS1826

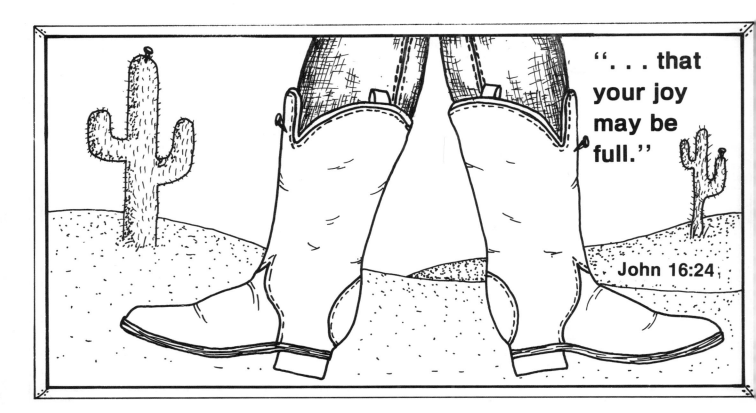

"...that your joy may be full."

John 16:24

DIRECTIONS:
Create this bulletin board with a colorful piece of material as a background. Use tan or another neutral color to coordinate with the fabric for the boots. Make the cactus from green construction paper. John 15:11 or John 16:24 are two good verses to use on this display.

IDEAS:
Use this display to announce a coming event. Title it "For a Real Kick . . . ." You could also use it to display students' work. Title the bulletin board "You'll Get a Real Kick out of Our Work in _____ Grade."

BONUS ACTIVITY:
Declare an upcoming day JOY DAY. Begin by having students make posters to announce the day and hang them around your church or school. Then have children make invitations inviting other classes to celebrate this day of JOY. Activities will depend on the age level you are working with. Make the children responsible for planning the fun-filled day.

ALTERNATIVE TITLES AND SCRIPTURE VERSES:
Rejoice!   I Pet. 4:13
Rejoice Evermore   I Thess. 5:16
Be Glad in the Lord   Ps. 32:11
Shout for Joy   Ps. 32:11
I Will Be Glad   Ps. 9:2
The Joy of the Lord   Neh. 8:10

48

SS1826

Work worth shouting about

DIRECTIONS:
Create this bulletin board using a printed fabric or a bright construction paper as a background. Create the computer with plain black paper or give it some extra character by using a bright color. You may choose to draw a front view of the computer, placing a cartoon face on the screen. See the cartoon faces found on page 93. Add a real plug from a discarded appliance. The border might be pages from a computer printout, cut in 3-4 inch strips.

IDEAS:
This bulletin board might be used to introduce computer terminology or for a learning center that includes computers.

BONUS ACTIVITY:
Have you hugged a student today? Giving praise to youngsters is one way to teach them to express praise. Take time to make some "praise" awards to pass out to all your students today.

ALTERNATIVE TITLES AND SCRIPTURE VERSES:
(Praise)

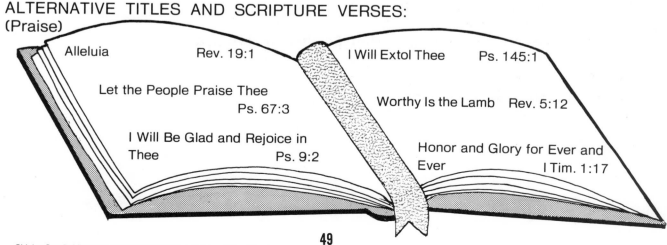

Alleluia Rev. 19:1	I Will Extol Thee Ps. 145:1
Let the People Praise Thee Ps. 67:3	Worthy Is the Lamb Rev. 5:12
I Will Be Glad and Rejoice in Thee Ps. 9:2	Honor and Glory for Ever and Ever I Tim. 1:17

SS1826

We're doing a WHALE of a job

DIRECTIONS:
Create this bulletin board using light blue for the water and white for the background. Use either gray or black for the happy whale. If you use black paper, do the highlights in white chalk. This could be the focal point for displaying student work.

IDEAS:
Use this same display to teach the story of Jonah, who was swallowed by a great fish. Study Jonah 1:1-17, especially 1:17.

BONUS ACTIVITY:
After the children are familiar with the story of Jonah, cut whale patterns from construction paper and attach them to Popsicle sticks. Encourage children to use the whale puppets to tell the story of Jonah.

ALTERNATIVE TITLES AND SCRIPTURE VERSES:
The Word of the Lord Came unto Jonah   Jonah 1:1
The Lot Fell upon Jonah   Jonah 1:7
They Took up Jonah, and Cast Him Forth into the Sea
     Jonah 1:15
Jonah Prayed unto the Lord   Jonah 2:1
Out of the Fish's Belly   Jonah 2:1

SS1826

DIRECTIONS:
Create this bulletin board with a light purple background. Use red for the strawberries and yellow-orange for the sun. Use Colossians 3:23 or Ecclesiastes 9:10 as the theme verse for this display. Challenge the students to strive for excellence and quality.

IDEAS:
Use this bulletin board as the starting point for an art project. Have the children draw and cut out cartoon fruits and vegetables to display on the board. See page 93 for cartoon faces. This board could also be titled "Berry Funny Fruit."

BONUS ACTIVITY:
Certain foods make us think of Bible stories. For example, bread reminds us of the Lord's Supper, while figs remind us of the parable of the fig tree. Challenge your Bible students to go on a Scripture picnic. As a group, make a list of as many foods as the children can find mentioned in the Bible. Then draw the shapes of each food on the appropriate color construction paper. Cut out the food shapes and write the appropriate Scripture verse on each. Display the shapes in a large basket drawn on the bulletin board.

SCRIPTURE VERSES THAT MENTION FOOD:
Fish—Matt. 17:27
Fig—Matt. 21:19
Fruit—Matt. 21:19
Bread—Matt. 26:26
Butter—Job 29:6
Meal—Luke 13:21
Honey—Gen. 43:11

SS1826

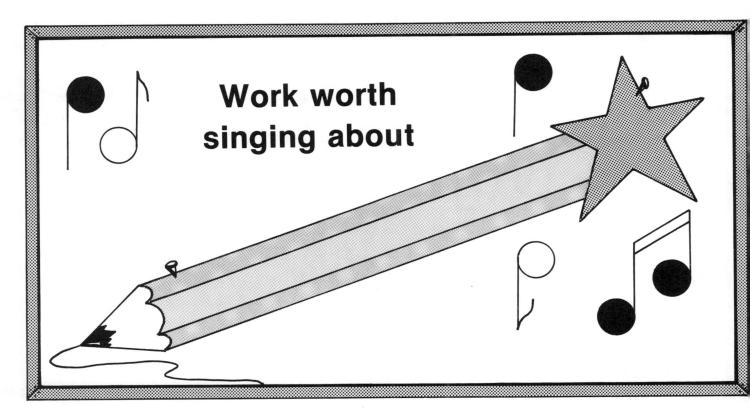

Work worth singing about

DIRECTIONS:
Create this bulletin board with a dark background, perhaps brown or blue. Use tan or orange for the pencil and yellow for the bright star. Use yarn to make writing "flow" from the pencil. Add colorful notes for appeal. This would be excellent for displaying handwriting improvements and exceptional papers with neat handwriting.

IDEAS:
You may want to use this bulletin board to list Bible verses that the children have memorized. Cut pencil-shaped awards from construction paper and pass them out every time a student learns a new verse.

BONUS ACTIVITY:
Encourage memory work by having children put Bible verses to familiar tunes. For example, if you change the verse slightly, Matthew 5:44 can be sung to the tune of "The Farmer in the Dell."

> Oh, love your enemies.
> Bless those who may curse you.
> Do good to them that hate
> And pray for all who do.

Or, Matthew 8:20 can be sung to "On Top of Old Smoky."

> The foxes have holes;
> Each bird has a nest.
> But the Son of man had
> No place he could rest.

The words do not have to be exact, but should be kept as near to Scripture as possible. See how many budding young songwriters you have in your class. After the songs have been arranged, be sure to sing them all!

          SS1826

Are you a reflection of Christ?

DIRECTIONS:
Create this bulletin board using green for the background, brown construction paper for the mirror frame and tinfoil for the glass in the mirror. There are many verses that could be used to illustrate this important principle from God's Word. As a class, discuss and list the reasons why we should be an acceptable reflection of Christ. You may want to use II Corinthians 3:18 as the theme verse for this bulletin board.

IDEAS:
Use this bulletin board to display self-portraits of the students.

BONUS ACTIVITY:
Take the self-portraits one step farther by having children make life-size outlines of themselves. Children will need to work with a partner. One child lies perfectly still on a sheet of butcher paper while his/her partner traces around his/her body. Then cut out, color, and decorate with pieces of material cut to resemble shirts, jeans, dresses, etc. Hang the life-size "children" around the classroom for everyone to admire.

ALTERNATIVE TITLES AND SCRIPTURE VERSES:
(Christ-Likeness)
We Shall Be like Him   I John 3:2
I Awake with Thy Likeness   Ps. 17:15
Beholding, as in a Mirror   II Cor. 3:18
Bear the Image of the Heavenly   I Cor. 15:49
Fashioned like unto His Glorious Body   Phil. 3:21

53

SS1826

Flying by with this important message

DIRECTIONS:
Create this bulletin board with a light blue background. Make the flying duck in any color or combination of colors for a real attention-getter. Add whatever message you choose.

IDEAS:
Use this bulletin board to highlight a study of ducks flying south in the fall. Bring in some duck decoys and a wood carver. You might also display some still life studies of ducks. This could be a very interesting enrichment activity.

BONUS ACTIVITY:
''Let your cares fly away'' is an expression often heard; but rarely is the advice taken. Help lighten the burdens your students may have by discussing how we can turn to God in prayer to take away our earthly cares. Then construct paper airplanes and have the children list on their airplanes something that is really bothering them. Take the planes outdoors for an afternoon of flying fun. Use the analogy of casting our cares to the wind to explain how we can pray about our problems and then trust God to take care of them for us.

ALTERNATIVE TITLES AND SCRIPTURE VERSES:
(Cares Of The World)
Cast All Your Cares upon God   I Pet. 5:7
Take Heed Lest Your Hearts Be Overcharged with the Cares
    of This Life   Luke 21:34
I Trust in the Lord   Ps. 31:6

SS1826

FOR A REAL TREAT

For a real treat . . . see what we've been learning . . .

Mrs. Young's Room

DIRECTIONS:
Create this bulletin board with a brightly printed fabric or wrapping paper as background. The individual candies should be made from construction paper. Use colors that complement the background. The candy kiss should be made from tinfoil. Identify the class on the white paper wrapper attached to the top of the kiss.

IDEAS:
Use this board to display student work.

BONUS ACTIVITY:
To really sweeten up learning in your classroom, attach real pieces of candy to the bulletin board. Each time a child memorizes an assigned Bible verse, he/she gets to choose a piece of candy from the board. Memory work is sure to soar!

ALTERNATIVE TITLES AND SCRIPTURE VERSES:
(Knowledge)

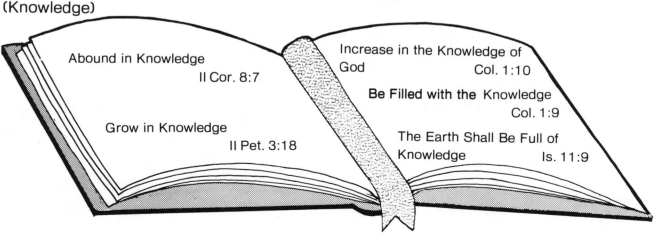

Abound in Knowledge
II Cor. 8:7

Grow in Knowledge
II Pet. 3:18

Increase in the Knowledge of God
Col. 1:10

Be Filled with the Knowledge
Col. 1:9

The Earth Shall Be Full of Knowledge
Is. 11:9

SS1826

YIELD

Yielding your new life to God

"Neither yield ye your members as instruments of unrighteousness unto sin: but yield yourselves unto God, as those that are alive from the dead, and your members as instruments of righteousness unto God."

Romans 6:13

DIRECTIONS:
Create this bulletin board with a bright background. The yield sign should be yellow, with lettering done by a black felt-tip marker.

IDEAS:
Do a brief study from Scripture of the things that we should yield to in our Christian life. One verse to use in this study is Hebrews 12:11. Brainstorm a class list of ideas and post them on the bulletin board.

BONUS ACTIVITY:
Children love mazes. Have each child create a "Life Maze." Children should place real-life obstacles on the maze paths. The correct path through the maze should contain words that help us in our daily Christian walk. Advice from parents, Scripture reading and prayer are good examples. Be sure to have the children title their mazes. You will learn many things about your students when you review their life mazes.

ALTERNATIVE TITLES AND SCRIPTURE VERSES:
(Life)
Walk in Newness   Rom. 6:4
Your Life Is Hid with Christ in God   Col. 3:3
I Am the Way, the Truth, and the Life   John 14:6

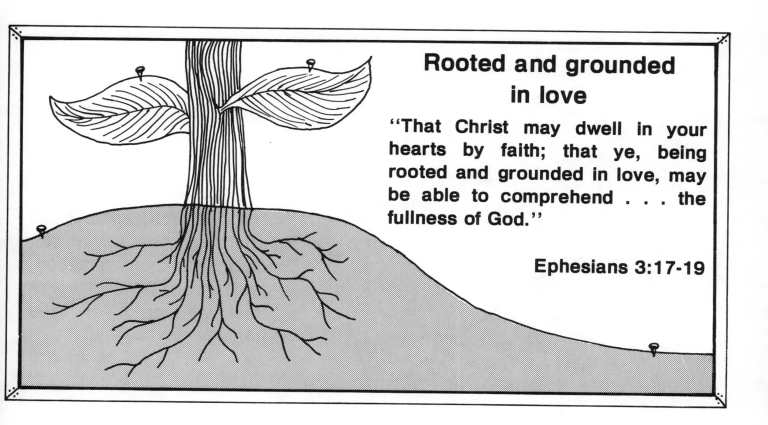

Rooted and grounded in love

"That Christ may dwell in your hearts by faith; that ye, being rooted and grounded in love, may be able to comprehend . . . the fullness of God."

Ephesians 3:17-19

DIRECTIONS:
Use a bright yellow for the background of this bulletin board. The stem and leaves of the plant should be bright green. The mound of earth should be tan. Draw the root of the plant with a felt-tip marker.

IDEAS:
Extend the plant up the wall of the classroom to the ceiling. Attach students' work to the plant. Title the board, "Our Good Work Just Keeps Growing." The plant could grow around the classroom walls.

BONUS ACTIVITY:
Turn the plant on this bulletin board into a tree of love. Instead of posting the children's work on the plant, place red hearts with Bible verses about LOVE. See who can find the word LOVE in the Bible the most times.

ALTERNATIVE TITLES AND SCRIPTURE VERSES:
(Love)
An Everlasting Love   Jer. 31:3
He First Loved Us   I John 4:19
Them That Love God   Rom. 8:28
Love the Lord Thy God   Matt. 22:37
Love Is Kind   I Cor. 13:4
Love Never Faileth   I Cor. 13:8
Let Us Love One Another   I John 4:7
Above All Things Put on Love   Col. 3:14

SS1826

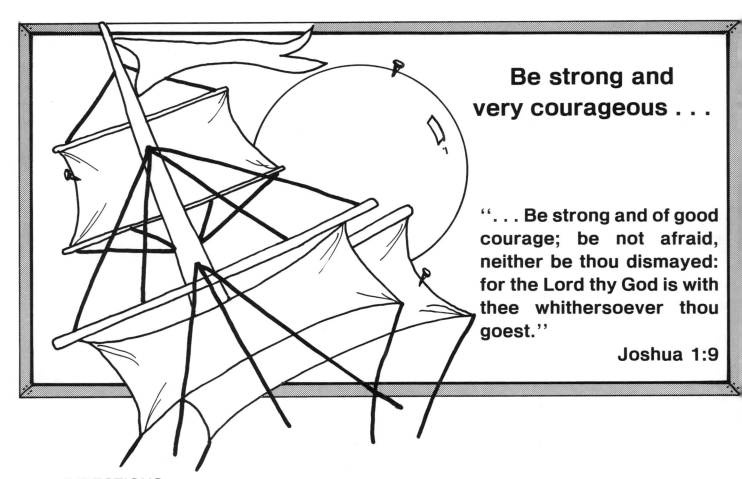

Be strong and very courageous . . .

". . . Be strong and of good courage; be not afraid, neither be thou dismayed: for the Lord thy God is with thee whithersoever thou goest."

Joshua 1:9

DIRECTIONS:
Create this appealing bulletin board with a light blue background. The large sun can be yellow or orange. The sails are white, the masts brown and the ropes tan. Use white muslin for one of the large sails for an extra-special 3-D display. The riggings can be actual twine or clothesline. Extend the upper and lower portions off the borders of your bulletin board. Make the ship's flag a bright cheerful color.

IDEAS:
This idea can be a springboard for a study of the Pilgrims and the struggles they endured on the trip to America, and also could honor Christopher Columbus.

BONUS ACTIVITY:
Use colored construction paper to create flags of courage. Let each child design his/her own flag with appropriate symbols of faith. Encourage children to choose Bible verses that will remind them to have courage; print them on their flags.

ALTERNATIVE TITLES AND SCRIPTURE VERSES:
(Fear Not)
Fear Not: They That Are with Us Are More than They That
    Are with Them   II Kin. 6:16
I Will Not Fear   Ps. 56:4
My Heart Shall Not Fear   Ps. 27:3
Be Not Afraid: Only Believe   Mark 5:36

58

SS1826

We all do fade as a leaf

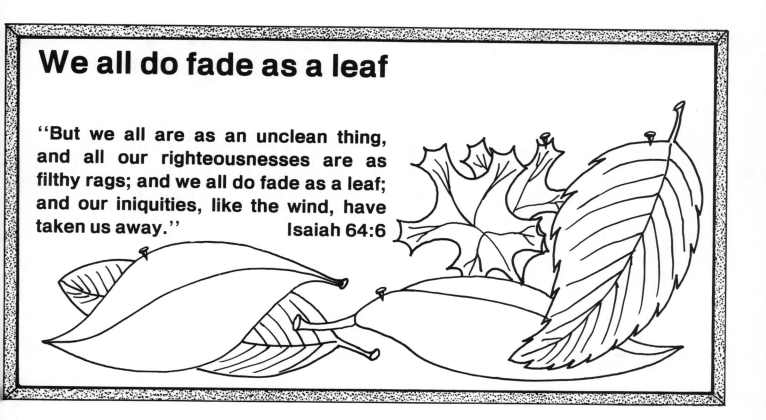

"But we all are as an unclean thing, and all our righteousnesses are as filthy rags; and we all do fade as a leaf; and our iniquities, like the wind, have taken us away."   Isaiah 64:6

DIRECTIONS:
Create this bulletin board using neutral-colored paper or use burlap for the background. Cut out leaves and mount them as shown above. Use fall foliage colors: red, orange, yellow and brown.

IDEAS:
Do a study of the Creator's fancy designs in nature. Why do leaves turn colors in the fall? Why do birds fly south? Why do bears hibernate? Make a list of some wonderfully complicated things that change in the autumn of the year.

BONUS ACTIVITY:
Reinforce this bulletin board by having the children do leaf rubbings. Take a hike around the playground or neighborhood to gather some leaves. Place a sheet of white paper on top of a leaf and rub the paper with the side of a crayon that has had the paper removed. Decorate the leaf rubbings with biblical phrases about redemption.

ALTERNATIVE TITLES AND SCRIPTURE VERSES:
(Redemption)
Your Redemption Draweth Nigh   Luke 21:28
Redeemed with Christ   I Pet. 1:19
Thou Hast Redeemed Us   Rev. 5:9

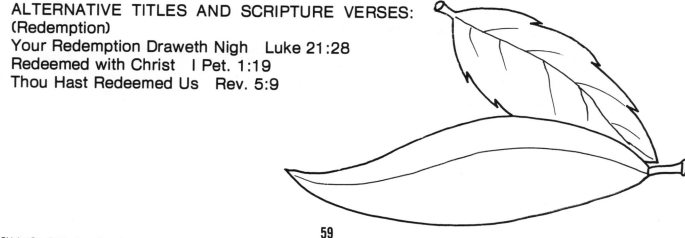

59

SS1826

A BUSHEL OF SPIRITUAL BLESSINGS

A bushel of spiritual blessings in heavenly places . . .

DIRECTIONS:
Create this board with a tan background. The bushel basket can be made from dark brown paper. Draw the details of the basket with felt-tip marker. Add fruit. On each of the fruits, list one of the blessings that God has given us through our Lord Jesus Christ.

IDEAS:
You may choose to use this board to welcome the students the first day of school. On each of the fruits, list the name of one of the students and place the fruit in the basket.

BONUS ACTIVITY:
''Orange'' you glad you know Jesus? We who know Jesus are truly blessed! Cut orange construction paper circles and use a black felt-tip pen to make the circles look like oranges. On the oranges have the children write prayers of thanks for the things with which they are blessed. Put the oranges in the basket on the board.

ALTERNATIVE TITLES AND SCRIPTURE VERSES:
(Blessedness)
Blessed Is He That Considereth the Poor   Ps. 41:1
Blessed Is the Man That Trusteth in the Lord   Ps. 34:8
Blessed Is the Nation Whose God Is the Lord   Ps. 33:12
Blessed Are They That Dwell in Thy House   Ps. 8:4
Blessed Are They That Hear the Word of God   Luke 11:28

SS1826

You'll get a real kick out of these . . .

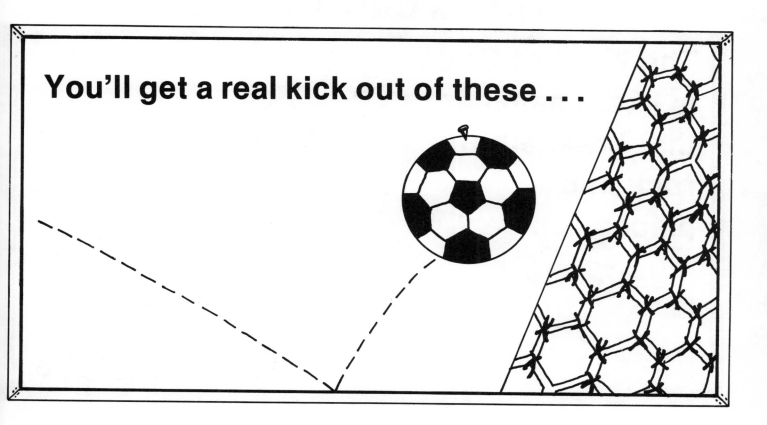

DIRECTIONS:
Make this bulletin board with either a light blue background or use some sporty wrapping paper. You can make the soccer ball the traditional black and white or combine your school colors. After the ball has been attached to the board, add the motion and bounce lines. Make the soccer net from white or tan paper. This simple display will allow plenty of room for messages or student work. It could be used to record the scores of teams involved in competitions or to list soccer rules.

IDEAS:
This board could also be used to keep track of sales or fund-raising campaigns in your school or church.

BONUS ACTIVITY:
Inspire student creative writing with a lesson entitled "Sporty Riddles." The students have to write riddles as if they were a piece of sports equipment. The riddle should not give the name of the game. Example: I've never been hit as hard as I was the last day of the season. What am I? (a baseball)

ALTERNATIVE TITLES AND SCRIPTURE VERSES:
(Championship with God)
Emmanuel, God with Us   Matt. 1:23
God Himself Is with Us for Our Captain   II Chr. 13:12
The Lord Stood with Me   II Tim. 4:17

61

THE WORD OF GOD

The word of God . . .
is like a hammer
that breaketh the
rock into
pieces . . .

DIRECTIONS:
Make this bulletin board with a bright yellow background. The handle of the hammer should be brown and the head of the hammer, gray or tinfoil. The rock can be tan. Add the cracks and splintering rock fragments with black marker.

IDEAS:
Remove the rock and add the head and shaft of a nail. Then you can title this board "We're Building Character." Use this board to display papers on Christian values or fruits of the Spirit.

BONUS ACTIVITY:
As a follow-up for this bulletin board, paint rocks to be used as paperweights. Encourage each student to paint a biblical symbol on his rock. Use small, smooth pebbles and acrylic paints.

ALTERNATIVE TITLES AND SCRIPTURE VERSES:
(Word)
Continue in My Word   John 8:31
Keep My Words   John 14:23
The Word of God Is Living and Powerful
     Heb. 4:12
My Words Shall Not Pass Away   Matt. 24:35
Wondrous Things out of Thy Law   Ps. 119:18

SS1826

WINTER

SS1826

WINTER WONDERLAND

God's   handiwork

DIRECTIONS:
Create this bulletin board using plain white paper for the background. Next add the evergreen tree, brown fencing, off-white or gray snowman, and aqua-blue hanging ice. Construct a window frame to stand out from the scene. Then add black or dark brown strips of construction paper to outline the window panes. Add a fabric scarf and hat, and twig arms to the snowman. Draw the rolling hills with felt-tip marker. You might even consider using Styrofoam balls that have been cut in half, for the body of the snowman.

IDEAS:
Have the children draw their own snowmen and display them on the bulletin board. You could also have your students create their own winter wonderland window scenes and display them around the edges of the bulletin board.

BONUS ACTIVITY:
Cut snowflakes to decorate the windows and walls of the classroom. For each snowflake, fold a sheet of white paper as if you are going to cut out a star. Then cut out small pieces along the folds and the edge of the folded paper. Unfold to discover a beautiful snowflake. No two will be the same.

Shining Star Publications, Copyright © 1987, A division of Good Apple, Inc.   SS1826

JOY TO THE WORLD

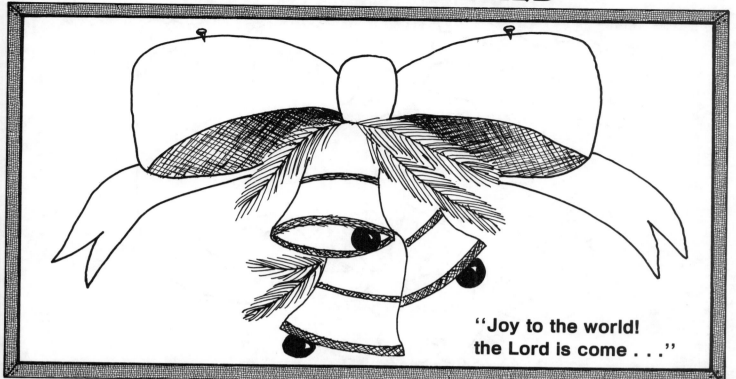

"Joy to the world!
the Lord is come . . ."

DIRECTIONS:
Create this bulletin board using red paper or Christmas wrapping paper for the background. Make the bells from tinfoil or gold and silver foil gift wrap. Use real ribbon for the borders. To complete the board, attach real evergreen branches or make some from green construction paper. This display is sure to create a feeling of great joy in your classroom. Celebrate Jesus' birth with these bells and glad tidings.

IDEAS:
You can use this bulletin board after the Christmas holidays by changing the title to read "Work Worth Ringing About."

BONUS ACTIVITY:
Use the bell theme of this bulletin board to make Christmas tree ornaments and gift package tags. Begin by cutting bell shapes from light cardboard. Then carefully cover both sides with foil or gold foil gift wrap and glue in place. Use a hole punch to make a small hole in the top of each bell. Attach a ribbon or a piece of yarn through the hole and secure with a bow. These bells can be hung on the tree or may be used to embellish Christmas packages.

ALTERNATIVE TITLES AND SCRIPTURE VERSES:
(Joy)
Be Glad in the Lord   Ps. 32:11
Enter into the Joy of the Lord   Matt. 25:21
Let Them Rejoice   Ps. 68:3
Rejoice with Joy Unspeakable and Full of Glory   I Pet. 1:8
Good Tidings of Great Joy   Luke 2:10

SS1826

GOOD TIDINGS OF GREAT JOY

DIRECTIONS:
Create this bulletin board to capture one of the very important words of Luke 2:10—JOY. Use light blue for the background. The letters can be created in a variety of ways. Try using cheerful wrapping paper in a combination of bright Christmas colors. Cap each of the letters with white construction-paper snow. Then either hang a large Christmas bow or create a 3-D bow from construction paper. Use Luke 2:10, ". . . Fear not: for, behold, I bring you good tidings of great joy . . ."

IDEAS:
God's Word is filled with reasons why our lives should be filled with joy. Some of these reasons include forgiveness, victory, faith and suffering. You might have your children draw angels to surround the display. On each angel write a word symbolizing joy.

BONUS ACTIVITY:
Use the pattern for the word JOY, found on the bulletin board, to make interesting-shaped Christmas cards. Cut around the outside shape of the letters, and fill in the details using black marking pens. If you want cards that open, place the pattern on paper that has been folded at the top. An appropriate Bible phrase about joy can be used inside.

ALTERNATIVE TITLES AND SCRIPTURE VERSES:
(Joy)
Let All Those That Seek Thee Rejoice   Ps. 70:4
Joy in the Holy Ghost   Rom. 14:17
Rejoice Because Your Names Are Written in Heaven
    Luke 10:20
Let Them Rejoice   Ps. 68:3
Shout for Joy   Ps. 5:11
I Will Rejoice in the Lord   Hab. 3:18

SS1826

God's love gift

"Therefore the Lord himself shall give you a sign; Behold, a virgin shall conceive, and bear a son, and shall call His name Immanuel."
Isaiah 7:14

". . . God with us." Matthew 1:23

DIRECTIONS:
Create this bulletin board with a bright wrapping paper background. The box can be created from blue, red, or green construction paper. You might consider using a real wrapped gift to create a 3-D effect. Make the ribbon and bow from the same wrapping paper design. This would be a good bulletin board to have beside your Chrismas tree in the classroom. Use it to illustrate the best gift that could have possibly been given by anyone—that of God's own Son, Jesus Christ. You can use the prophetic account of Christ's birth as found in Isaiah 7:14 and then add the fulfillment (Matthew 1:23).

IDEAS:
Use this board after Christmas by changing the title to read "The Gift of Yourself." Attach essays on subjects such as kindness, loyalty, trustworthiness, love, etc. Romans 12:21, "Be not overcome of evil, but overcome evil with good," is an appropriate Scripture verse for this new board.

BONUS ACTIVITY:
Your class can create a booklet called "Gifts for God." Hand out a creative writing work sheet in the shape of a gift. Have the children write or draw pictures of things they would like to give God this Christmas. Then compile all the stories into a book and put a cover on it. Donate the book to the school or church library.

ALTERNATIVE TITLES AND SCRIPTURE VERSES:
(Gifts)
My Peace I Give unto You   John 14:27
The Gift of God Is Eternal Life   Rom. 6:23
God Loveth a Cheerful Giver   II Cor. 9:7

Every Man Shall Give as He Is Able
Deut. 16:17
Give, and It Shall Be Given unto You
Luke 6:38

SS1826

SO TEACH US TO NUMBER OUR DAYS

"So teach us to number our days, that we may apply our hearts unto wisdom."

Psalm 90:12

DIRECTIONS:
Construct this bulletin board with a bright piece of printed material or wrapping paper for the background. Use a coordinating color for the timepieces. Use Colossians 4:5 as an additional reference for this display.

IDEAS:
Use this bulletin board as a springboard for doing a Bible study about time. Encourage the children to write Bible trivia questions based on time. Example: How old was Noah when he built the ark? How old was Sarah when she had her son?

BONUS ACTIVITY:
Have each child create a pictorial time line of his/her life so far. The students should illustrate important events, such as learning to crawl, learning to walk, learning to ride a bike, going to school, losing the first tooth, etc.

ALTERNATIVE TITLES AND SCRIPTURE VERSES:
(Wisdom)
Be Wise as Serpents   Matt. 10:16
In Christ Are Hid the Treasures of Wisdom   Col. 2:3
Walk in Wisdom   Col. 4:5
Let the Word of Christ Dwell in You Richly in All Wisdom
     Col. 3:16
Wisdom Is More Precious than Rubies   Prov. 3:15

Shining Star Publications, Copyright © 1987, A division of Good Apple, Inc.

SS1826

PRAISE YE THE LORD

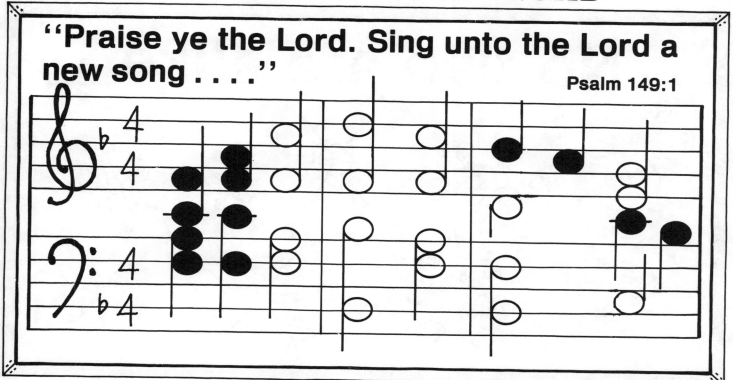

"Praise ye the Lord. Sing unto the Lord a new song . . . ."

Psalm 149:1

DIRECTIONS:
Create this bulletin board using a brightly printed fabric with the notes in a coordinating color. Use Psalm 149:1 as the Scripture selection for this display. Add other musical symbols if you wish.

IDEAS:
Use this simple display for the music classroom or during a music week at your school. Ephesians 5:19 is another excellent choice for the Scripture selection for this display. See if you can find other Scriptures to add to this display.

BONUS ACTIVITY:
Encourage your students to think about their uniqueness by having them write simple six-line poems with seven syllables to each line, that describe themselves. Then have them put their poems to music by singing them to the tune of "Twinkle, Twinkle, Little Star."

> Example:
> My name is Amy Daniel.
> I have a cocker spaniel.
> My mother says that I'm smart.
> My favorite subject is art.
> My favorite color is blue.
> I play a violin, too!

ALTERNATIVE TITLES AND SCRIPTURE VERSES:
(Singing)
Sing unto God   Ps. 68:32
Let Us Sing   Ps. 95:1
I Will Sing Aloud   Ps. 59:16
Melody in Your Heart   Eph. 5:19

SS1826

No two are alike

DIRECTIONS:
Construct this bulletin board using a light blue background. Make the snowflakes from white construction paper, using the instructions found on page 64. Let your class create a variety of patterns for the display. Job 37:6 can be used as a Scripture idea.

IDEAS:
This may be a good springboard for a class discussion about each individual's uniqueness. Like snowflakes, no two people are exactly alike. It is also a good way to illustrate the greatness of God the Creator.

BONUS ACTIVITY:
Make this bulletin board a real hit with all the children by attaching a photograph of each student to the center of a snowflake. Title this bulletin board ''All Things Were Made by Him . . .'' (John 1:3).

ALTERNATIVE TITLES AND SCRIPTURE VERSES:
(God as the Creator)
God Created Man in His Own Image   Gen. 1:27
And They Were Created   Ps. 148:5
We Are His Workmanship   Eph. 2:10
By Him Were All Things Created   Col. 1:16

SS1826

THE FOWLS OF THE HEAVENS

". . . The fowls of the heaven have their habitation . . . ."

Psalm 104:12

DIRECTIONS:
Create this bulletin board using a light blue background. Use green for the pine needles and white for the snow. For a 3-D display, use real pine branches and spray them with artificial snow. The chickadee can be grayish-white with a black cap. Use Psalm 104:12 for the Scripture selection on this bulletin board.

IDEAS:
This display might be an attractive bulletin board to use in conjunction with your winter calendar. Use the same verse but different birds and trimmings to depict the various seasons. For example, a robin in a tree with apple blossoms might represent spring.

BONUS ACTIVITY:
Building a nest may seem like a simple task; maybe it is for a bird. Challenge your students to build a better nest than a bird can build. (Remember, birds don't even have hands to work with.) Allow the children to use any materials they choose. Place a time limit of one evening at home to create their bird nests. Award a prize for the best built.

ALTERNATIVE TITLES AND SCRIPTURE VERSES:
(Heavenly Home)
Your Names Are Written in Heaven   Luke 10:20
In My Father's House Are Many Mansions   John 14:2
A House Not Made with Hands   II Cor. 5:1
Reserved in Heaven for You   I Pet. 1:11

SS1826

DIRECTIONS:
Create this bulletin board using an orange background. Use brown or tan construction paper to make the roaring lion. I Peter 5:8 can be used as a caption.

IDEAS:
Use this bulletin board to announce an important coming event. You could title it ''Now Hear This . . .'' Or ''For a Roaring Good Time . . .'' List the details of the event and place it where everyone will be able to take notice. You could also display student class work with the title ''Here Is Our Work That Is Worth Roaring About.''

BONUS ACTIVITY:
Let your fingers do the walking through the Scriptures. Challenge your students to list all the ways the Bible tells them to walk. Example: Walk in love (Eph. 5:2). A list of other suggestions is included below. Put each of these Bible-based phrases on construction paper footprints and attach them to the ceiling of your classroom: walk honestly, I Thess. 4:12; walk in Christ, Col. 2:6; walk uprightly, Prov. 2:7; walk in wisdom, Col. 4:5; walk in my law, Ex. 16:4; walk before God, Gen. 17:1; walk in the light, I John 1:7; walk in truth, III John 4; walk in the Spirit, Gal. 5:16; walk in his paths, Is. 2:3; walk in integrity, Ps. 26:11; walk after the Lord, Hos. 11:10; walk before me for ever, I Sam. 2:30; walk in newness of life, Rom. 6:4; walk worthy of the Lord, Col. 1:10; walk in the name of the Lord, Mic. 4:5; walk after his commandments, II John 6; walk in the way of good men, Prov. 2:20; walk in all the ways of the Lord, Deut. 5:33; walk in the light of thy countenance, Ps. 89:15; walk in all the ways I command you, Jer. 7:23; walk before thee with all their heart, I Kin. 8:23; walk in my house with a perfect heart, Ps. 101:2.

SS1826

Bad habits are highway robbery

DIRECTIONS:
Create this bulletin board with a bright background, such as yellow or orange. The hat can be brown, the face flesh color, and the handkerchief could be made from red paper or cloth. List bad habits around the edges of the board. Use Jeremiah 13:23 as the Scripture reference for this display.

IDEAS:
You could use this display for teaching a unit on good nutrition. Title it ''Poor Eating Habits Rob YOU of Your Health.'' Display healthy and unhealthy foods on each side of the bandit. There are many other ways that you might use this figure. Let your imagination go!

BONUS ACTIVITY:
Have children keep a journal for one day to determine how they spend most of their time. Does television rob them of their lives? What percentage of their time is spent reading? studying? Graph the results. Or have students record what they eat for three days. Discuss the menus.

ALTERNATIVE TITLES AND SCRIPTURE VERSES:
(Deceiving)
Take Heed That No Man Deceive You   Matt. 24:4
Let No Man Deceive You with Vain Words   Eph. 5:6
Many Deceivers Are Entered into the World   II John 7

73

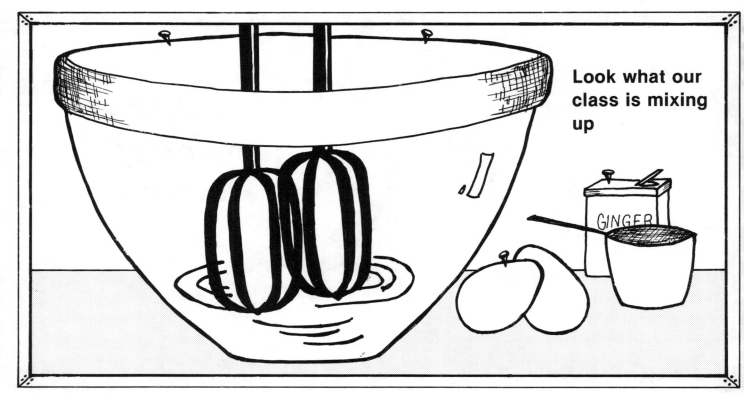

Look what our class is mixing up

DIRECTIONS:
Create this bulletin board using a red gingham or a paper tablecloth. Make the mixing bowl and eggs from white paper, the beaters from black. After the bowl and beaters are attached to the display, draw the motion lines. You may want to add other baking items, such as measuring cups, spoons, spices, etc., to the display.

IDEAS:
Use this bulletin board to display student work. Or display recipes without titles. The children must try to figure out the name of the recipe by reading the ingredients.

BONUS ACTIVITY:
Have the children write recipes for LOVE, FRIENDSHIP or any other Christian value.
    Example: Recipe for Friendship
    1 bushel of love
    1 armful of hugs
    1 dash of patience
    stir and bake slowly for many years

ALTERNATIVE TITLES AND SCRIPTURE VERSES:
(Fruit of the Spirit)
Be Gentle   Titus 3:2
Precious Faith   II Pet. 1:1
Fruit of the Spirit Is Goodness   Gal. 5:22
Humble Yourself   I Pet. 5:6
The Joy of the Lord   Neh. 8:10
He Is Kind   Luke 6:35
Put on a Heart of Longsuffering   Col. 3:12
Above All Things Have Love   I Pet. 4:8
Follow Peace   Heb. 12:14

74

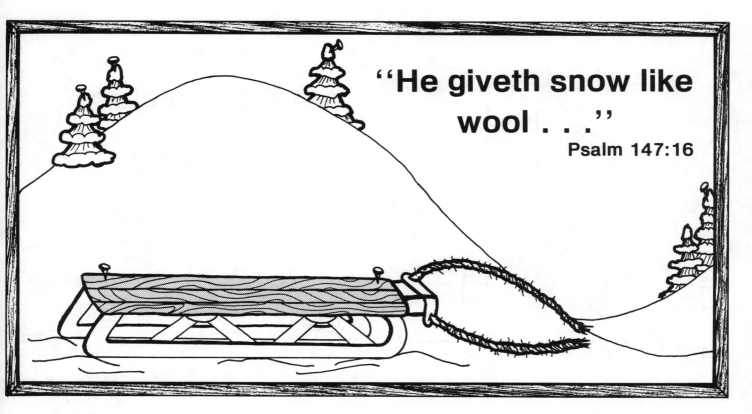

"He giveth snow like wool . . ."

Psalm 147:16

DIRECTIONS:
Create this display using white for the background. Make the sled from red paper and the rope from brown paper, or use a real piece of rope. Add small evergreen branches to make the trees in the background, or use green paper. Load the sled with any appropriate objects to complete this display.

IDEAS:
Nothing seems to be as quiet as falling snow. Spend a few minutes sitting quietly listening as snow falls.

BONUS ACTIVITY:
Ask the children to think about quiet gifts, and then illustrate or cut out pictures of some and load them on the sled on this bulletin board. Title the board "Quiet Gifts."

ALTERNATIVE TITLES AND SCRIPTURE VERSES:
(Quietness)

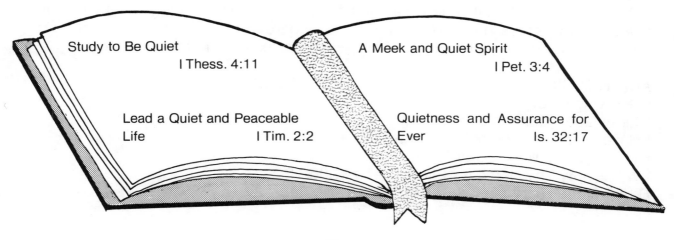

Study to Be Quiet
I Thess. 4:11

A Meek and Quiet Spirit
I Pet. 3:4

Lead a Quiet and Peaceable Life
I Tim. 2:2

Quietness and Assurance for Ever
Is. 32:17

SS1826

" . . . the whole earth is full of his glory."

Isaiah 6:3

DIRECTIONS:
Cover the entire bulletin board with light blue paper for the background. The barn is to be made from red construction paper and the silo from brown. Add evergreen trees in the background as well as one large tree off to the left side in the foreground. Use a black felt-tip marker to fill in the fence, the wood grain on the barn, and to draw the hillsides and other details of this bulletin board. Don't forget the weather vane on top of the barn. Spray artificial snow on the ground and on the rooftop to complete this beautiful winter scene.

IDEAS:
Have the children put glitter on the snow, on the trees and on the rooftop to add sparkle to the display.

BONUS ACTIVITY:
Glorify His name! In more than one hundred fifty places in the four Gospels Jesus speaks of God as ''Father,'' My Father,'' ''Our Father,'' ''Thy Father,'' ''Righteous Father.'' Have each child choose a name for God from the Bible and carefully print the name in box letters on a piece of light cardboard. Spread glue on the letters and sprinkle glitter on the glue. Post the sparkling names around the classroom.

ALTERNATIVE TITLES AND SCRIPTURE VERSES:
(Glorifying God)
Glorify God   Cor. 6:20
I Have Glorified Thee on the Earth   John 17:4
By Your Good Works Glorify God   I Pet. 2:12
I Will Glorify Thy Name for Evermore   Ps. 86:12
Do All to the Glory of God   I Cor. 10:31

SS1826

PETER PENGUIN SAYS

Walk with grace

DIRECTIONS:
Construct this bulletin board with a white background. The hanging ice should be made with light blue construction paper. The penguin can be drawn on white paper and filled in with india ink or black felt-tip marker. Add a real stocking hat and scarf for some interest and humor.

IDEAS:
Use this display for student work, winter safety tips or a winter calendar of events.

BONUS ACTIVITY:
Penguins are well known for their special kind of walk. It may not be described as graceful, but it works for penguins. Play a guessing game with the children to liven up any cold winter afternoon. The children are to take turns pantomiming the way different animals walk. When someone guesses the correct animal, he or she gets to be next.

ALTERNATIVE TITLES AND SCRIPTURE VERSES:
(Grace)
Grow in Grace   II Pet. 3:18
Singing with Grace   Col. 3:16
The God of All Grace   I Pet. 5:10
The Glory of His Grace   Eph. 1:6
Grace to You and Peace from God   Rom. 1:7

Shining Star Publications, Copyright © 1987, A division of Good Apple, Inc.

SS1826

FRIENDS

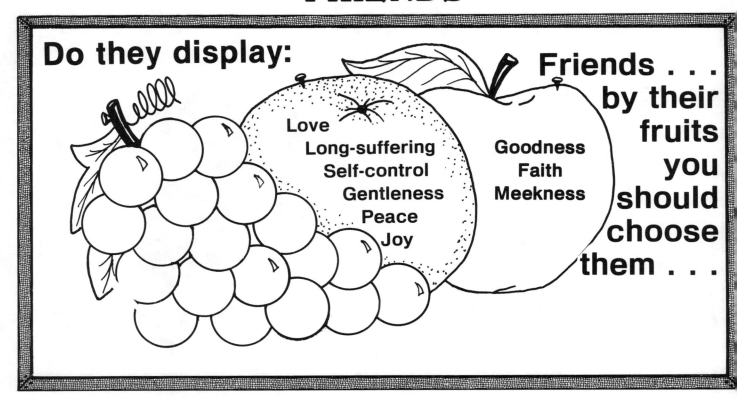

Do they display:

Love
Long-suffering
Self-control
Gentleness
Peace
Joy

Goodness
Faith
Meekness

Friends . . . by their fruits you should choose them . . .

DIRECTIONS:
Construct this bulletin board on a bright yellow background. Make each of the pieces of fruit the appropriate color. This board offers a very important message for young people. Peer pressure is very strong, and it is often hard to choose friends wisely.

IDEAS:
After doing an in-depth study of John 15, brainstorm a list of adjectives that describe a good friend. Attach the list to the bulletin board.

BONUS ACTIVITY:
Have the children use all the words on the list to create a word-search puzzle. Exchange papers and have the students complete each others' puzzles.

ALTERNATIVE TITLES AND SCRIPTURE VERSES:
(Children)

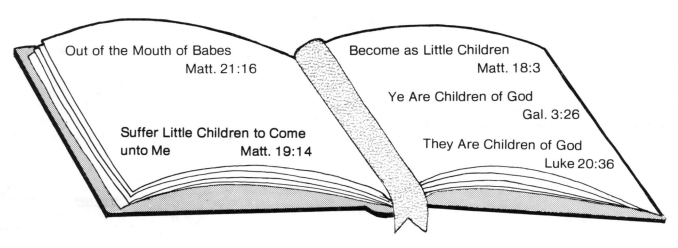

Out of the Mouth of Babes
Matt. 21:16

Suffer Little Children to Come unto Me   Matt. 19:14

Become as Little Children
Matt. 18:3

Ye Are Children of God
Gal. 3:26

They Are Children of God
Luke 20:36

SS1826

Shoveling our way into . . .

DIRECTIONS:
Make this bulletin board with a light blue construction paper background. Use white paper for the snow in the foreground. The shovel can be made from any color you choose. Add evergreen trees. Sometimes winter seems like it will never pass. Use this board to introduce Scripture verses about FAITH.

IDEAS:
You can use this board to display illustrations, sayings, recipes, riddles, etc., about winter snow.

BONUS ACTIVITY:
As a class, make a list of ways students can help older people during the winter months. Examples: shoveling snow, running errands when it's icy or baking special treats. On paper snowballs have each child write goals for helping two or three elderly friends. Attach the snowballs to the board. As the deeds are completed, have the students share experiences with the class and remove the snowballs from the bulletin board. When the good deeds are completed, the snow will all be shoveled.

ALTERNATIVE TITLES AND SCRIPTURE VERSES:
(Faith)
Work of Faith   I Thess. 1:3
Precious Faith   II Pet. 1:1
By Faith Ye Stand   II Cor. 1:24
Faith Works by Love   Gal. 5:6
Faith Without Works Is Dead   James 2:20

79

SS1826

OUT OF YOUR MOUTH

"Let no corrupt communication proceed out of your mouth, but that which is good to the use of edifying, that it may minister grace unto the hearers."

Ephesians 4:29

DIRECTIONS:
Make this bulletin board using a brightly printed fabric for the background. Make the telephone from a coordinating color.

IDEAS:
Encourage the children to use the phone to cheer up people who may be alone a lot. The Bible says we are to HEAR the Word and then share it. As a class, list some Bible verses about hearing and sharing the Word with others.

BONUS ACTIVITY:
Have the children memorize one Bible verse about hearing the Word. Then have them call people they know and share this verse with them. Have them keep track of the number of people they contact during one week. This could be a class competition.

ALTERNATIVE TITLES AND SCRIPTURE VERSES:
(Hearing)

Heareth God's Words
John 8:47

Hear the Word of the Lord
Jer. 22:29

If Any Man Have Ears to Hear, Let Him Hear
Mark 4:23

Blessed Is He That Hear the Words
Rev. 1:3

SS1826

WALKING ON THIN ICE

"Keeping evil company is like walking on thin ice . . . sooner or later you FALL

DIRECTIONS:
Make this bulletin board with a white and light blue background. The snow bank can be drawn on with felt-tip marker. Make the sign from tan construction paper. After you attach the sign to the board, add the crack lines in the ice. I Corinthians 15:33 may be used as a Scripture reference.

IDEAS:
Ice safety rules can be posted on this board during the winter months.

BONUS ACTIVITY:
Have the children make other signs for this bulletin board. Cut construction paper signs and carefully print biblical phrases that teach that we are safe when we are guided by God.

ALTERNATIVE TITLES AND SCRIPTURE VERSES:
He Led Them on Safely   Ps. 78:53
Lead Us Not into Temptation   Matt. 6:13
Thou Wilt Show Me the Path of Life   Ps. 16:11
He Will Be Our Guide   Ps. 48:14
The Lord Shall Guide Thee Continually
     Is. 58:11
The Lord Guided Them on Every Side
     II Chr. 32:22
Lead Me, Guide Me   Ps. 31:3

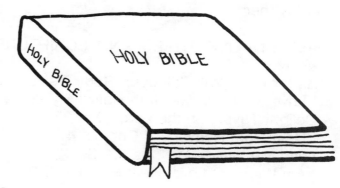

SS1826

THE LORD SHALL GIVE YOU A SIGN

"Therefore the Lord himself shall give you a sign; Behold, a virgin shall conceive, and bear a son, and shall call his name Immanuel."

Isaiah 7:14

"For unto us a child is born, unto us a son is given . . ."

Isaiah 9:6

DIRECTIONS:
Create this bulletin board with white for the background. The Christmas ornament can be made from yellow or light blue paper. Color the holly green and the ribbon red. The manger should be brown. The lettering and small details can be drawn on the board with a felt-tip marker.

IDEAS:
Have each child draw and cut out his own Christmas ornament. This may be a good opportunity for a Christmas art contest. Display all the ornaments on the board and let someone judge the best ones. Award prizes for the most creative ornaments.

BONUS ACTIVITY:
After a study of Bible verses about prayer, have the children write rhyming prayers based on the verses which they have studied.
Example:
        Lord, lead me and guide me.
        O Lord, how I love Thee.

Display all the rhyming prayers on the bulletin board so classroom visitors can read and enjoy them.

ALTERNATIVE TITLES AND SCRIPTURE VERSES:
(Prayer)
As for Me, I Will Call upon God   Ps. 55:16
I Love the Lord, He Hath Heard My Voice   Ps. 116:1
Delight Thyself in the Lord   Ps. 37:4
I Hear from Heaven   II Chr. 7:14
Lead Me, Guide Me   Ps. 31:3
I Am Weak, O Lord, Heal Me   Ps. 6:2

SS1826

4

7

8

5

7

6

9

10

15

11

16

12

17

13

18

14

CAUTION

SPRING

19

20

26

22

21

25

24

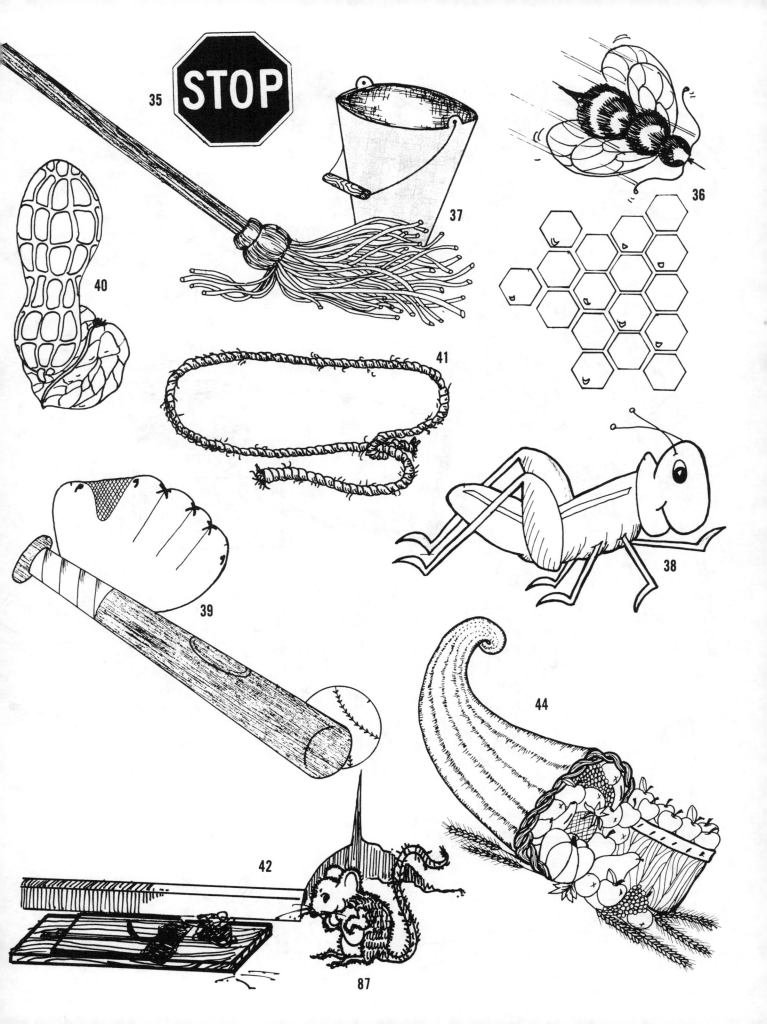

35

STOP

37

36

40

41

39

38

44

42

87

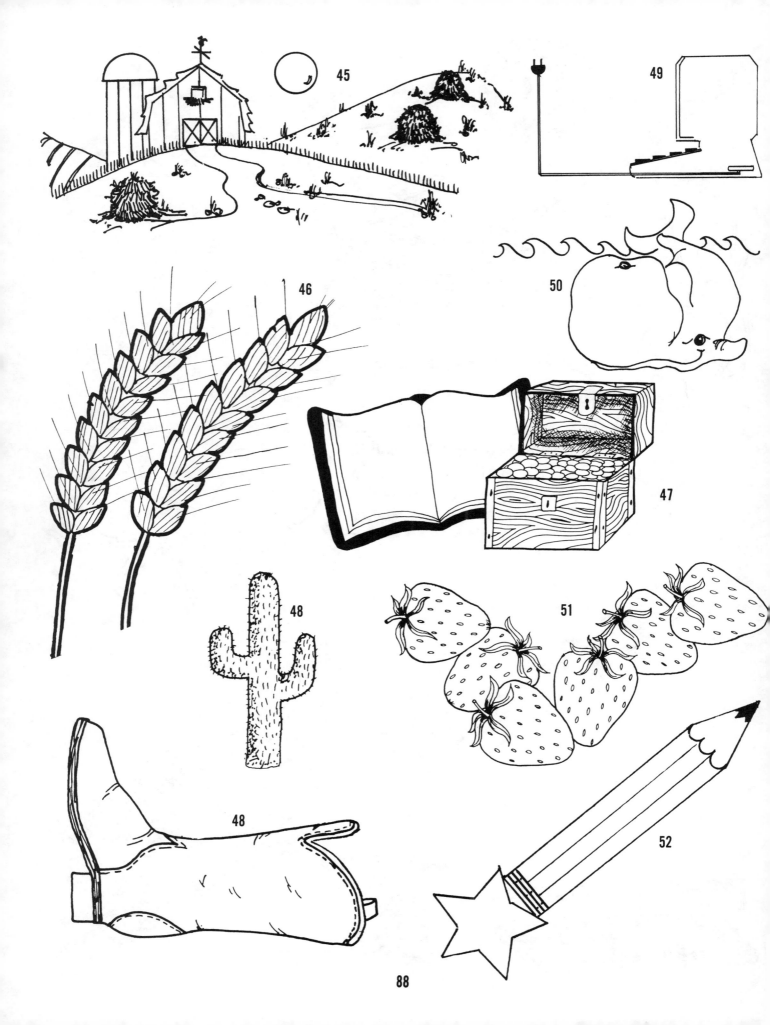

45

49

46

50

47

48

51

48

52

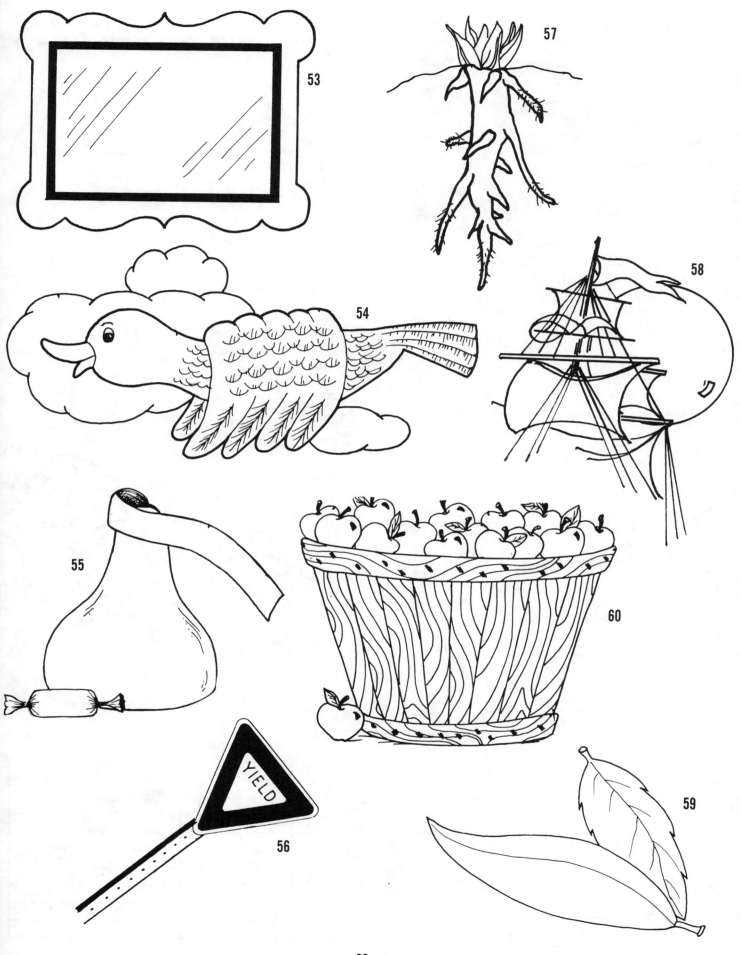

53

57

54

58

55

60

56

YIELD

59

61

66

62

65

64

68

67

69

70

72

76

71

73

74

76

75

91

You may add these facial features to the subjects that you use on the bulletin boards. You might create just the right expression on your next display figure!

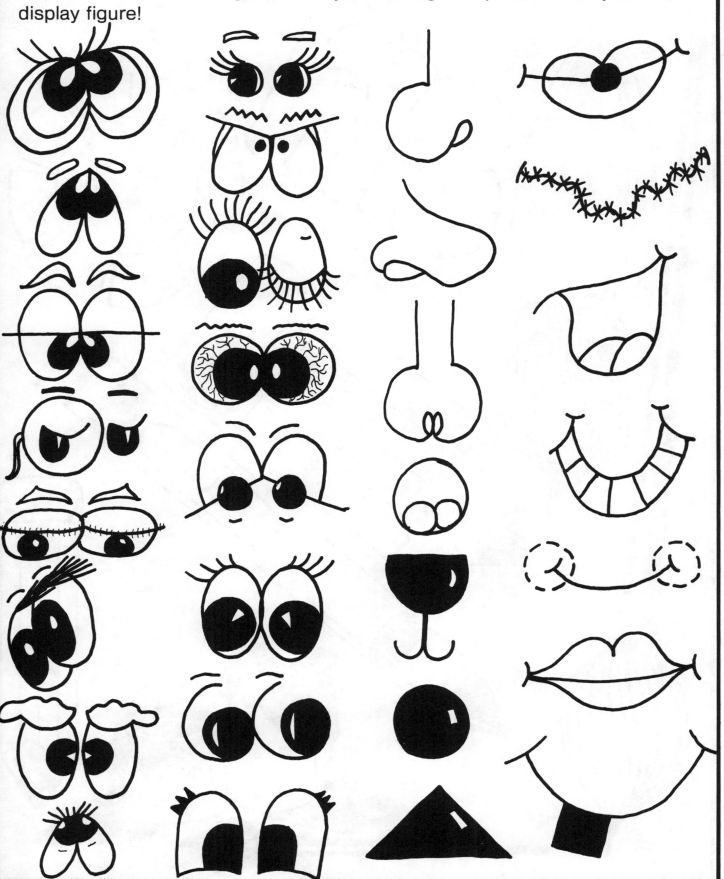

SS1826

CLIP ART

94

SS1826

CLASSROOM CLOCKS

DIRECTIONS: Try something different with the clock in your classroom. Cut out the eyes, smile, and the bow tie. Using masking tape, attach the pieces to the face of your clock. Add yellow or orange sunbeams extending outward from the clock frame—it really becomes a conversation piece. The bow tie can be attached as illustrated. On the following pages are seasonal variations for the clock face.

SS1826

CLOCK VARIATIONS:

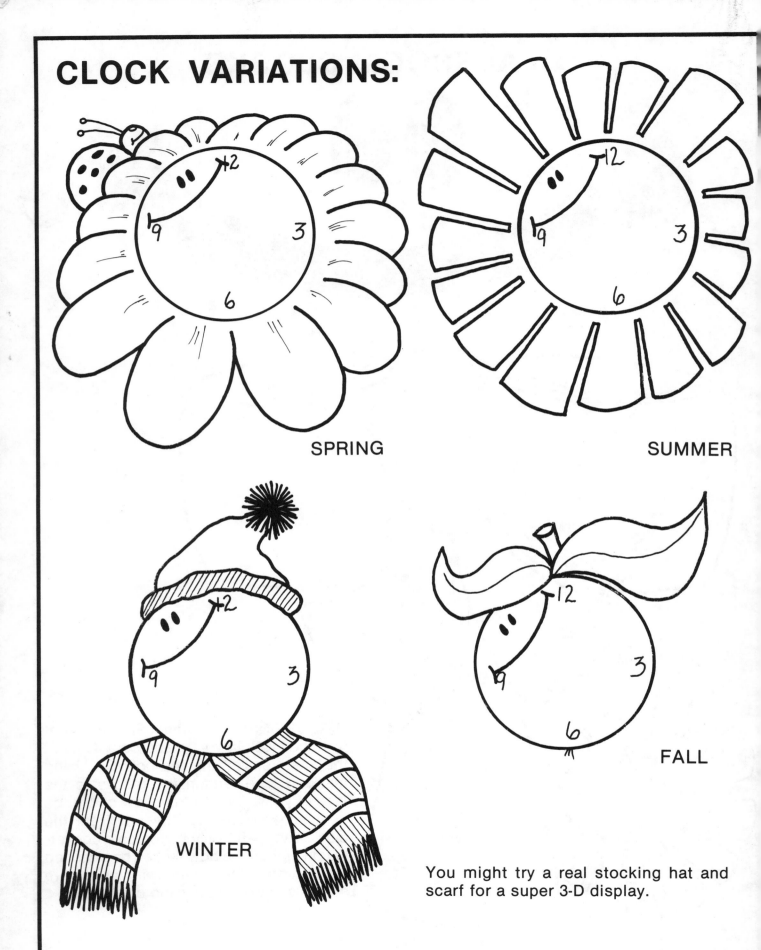

SPRING

SUMMER

WINTER

FALL

You might try a real stocking hat and scarf for a super 3-D display.

96

SS1826